RECEPTION BIN×GO

MW00813394

SOMEONE SHOUT-SINGS ALONG TO EVERY SONG & NEVER KNOWS THE WORDS.	A GIRL GETS BODY-CHECKED DURING THE BOUQUET TOSS.	'SO, HOW LONG DO YOU THINK THIS ONE WILL LAST?'	SOMEONE GETS CAKE RELENTLESSLY SMASHED IN THEIR FACE.	THE FATHER DAUGHTER DANCE MUSIC IS A BIT TOO ROMANTIC.
A MEMBER OF THE WEDDING PARTY VOMITS.	A BORED 5-YEAR-OLD JUST LAYS IN THE MIDDLE OF THE FLOOR.	SOMEONE IS EATING AN UNGODLY AMOUNT OF CHEESE.	2 HOURS IN & SOMEONE STILL HASN'T STOPPED CRYING.	A DISTANT RELATIVE CLOSE-TALKS WITH THE COUPLE FOR 30 MINUTES.
'I REMEMBER THE NIGHT YOU MET' IS SAID DURING A SPEECH.	DRUNK BROS START PUNCHING EACH OTHER TO SHOW AFFECTION.		SOMEONE WON'T STOP CHANTING 'KISS! KISS! KISS!' AT THE COUPLE.	AN OLDER COUPLE STARTS DIRTY DANCING TO A MODERN SONG.
THE WEDDING DJ PRONOUNCES SOMEONE'S NAME WRONG.	SOMEONE HAS ON WAY TOO MUCH PERFUME / COLOGNE.	ABSOLUTELY NO ONE KNOWS WHO ONE OF THE GUESTS IS.	THE CAKE TOPPERS ARE DISNEY CHARACTERS.	A CHRONIC DANCER IS SWEATING PROFUSELY.
'WOOOO!!' IS DRUNKENLY YELLED IN OTHERWISE SILENCE.	A POTENTIAL FIST FIGHT ENDS IN AGGRESSIVE HUGGING.	THE BRIDE STARTS WALKING AROUND BAREFOOT.	AN OLDER GRANDPARENT AND / OR DRUNK UNCLE FALLS ASLEEP AT A TABLE.	THE COUPLE IS INTRODUCED TO THE THEME OF 'ROCKY' OR SOME CRAP.

OBJECTIVE

OH, YOU MEAN BESIDES TRYING TO PASS THE TIME DURING THIS WEDDING THAT YOU MAY OR MAY NOT HAVE EVEN WANTED TO GO TO? ISN'T THAT ENOUGH? WHAT DO YOU WANT FROM US?

WELL, WE HOPE YOU'RE AT LEAST FAMILIAR WITH THE CONCEPT OF BINGO. BECAUSE IF NOT, WELL WE ARE REALLY KIND OF WORRIED ABOUT YOU. WHAT OTHER THINGS IN LIFE HAVE YOU MISSED? SHOES? AUTOMOBILES? TWO-PLY TOILET PAPER? WE DIGRESS.

THIS WEDDING BIN·GO GAME IS PLAYED MUCH LIKE THE TRADITIONAL ONE. YOUR GOAL IS TO SIMPLY BE THE FIRST TO FILL 5 SEQUENTIAL SQUARES IN A ROW, A COLUMN, OR EVEN DIAGONALLY (SEE FIGURE 1 BELOW).

FIGURE 1

SEE THAT X IN THE CENTER SQUARE OF YOUR BOARDS? THAT'S A FREE SQUARE—WHICH MEANS EVERY PLAYER GETS THIS ONE AUTOMATICALLY. IT REALLY HELPS SO...YOU'RE WELCOME

PLAYING THE GAME

AFTER DETERMINING HOW MANY PEOPLE ARE PLAYING, THE OWNER OF THE BOOK SHOULD PERF. OUT A CARD (OR TWO) FOR EVERYONE TO USE AS THEIR PLAY BOARD(S).

ALRIGHT, SO HERE'S HOW OUR GAME IS A BIT DIFFERENT. WE'VE PRE-FILLED EACH CARD WITH THE COMMON (YET RIDICULOUS) THINGS THAT ALWAYS SEEM TO HAPPEN AT THESE EVENTS. SO, INSTEAD OF SOMEONE JUST CALLING OUT NUMBERS, EVERYONE IS PEOPLE WATCHING INSTEAD. WHEN SOMETHING HAPPENS THAT IS ON ONE OF YOUR SQUARES, YOU CALL IT OUT* (AS DISCREETLY AS APPROPRIATE, OF COURSE) AND MARK OFF THE SQUARE. JUST MAKE SURE THE OTHER PLAYERS ARE AWARE.

BY THE WAY, BRIDES & GROOMS TEND TO DO UNIQUELY STUPID THINGS, SO WE PUT THEM IN. ATTENDING A SAME SEX MARRIAGE? AWESOME. FEEL FREE TO MODIFY THE SQUARES AS NEEDED.

WINNING

WHEN A PLAYER MARKS OFF A WINNING CARD, THEY SHOULD YELL* 'BINGO.' IN THE EVENT OF A TIE, THE FIRST TO SAY IT IS THE WINNER. EITHER WAY—EVERYONE ELSE IN THE ROOM WILL PROBABLY BE WONDERING WHAT THE HELL YOU ARE DOING. ADMITTEDLY IT MIGHT BE HARD TO MAKE A TRUE BINGO, SO YOU CAN ALSO DECIDE THAT THE PLAYER WITH THE MOST SQUARES MARKED OFF IS THE WINNER.

BONUS: YOU CAN ALSO PLAY THIS AS A DRINKING GAME. IT'S SIMPLE. WHEN SOMETHING HAPPENS ON YOUR CARD, YOU HAVE TO TAKE A DRINK. IF YOU MAKE A BINGO—WELL NOW EVERYONE ELSE HAS TO DRINK. JUST MAYBE WAIT UNTIL THE RECEPTION TO START DRINKING. THAT'S WHERE THE OPEN BAR IS ANYWAY.

*DON'T ACTUALLY YELL (OR TALK) DURING A WEDDING.

BIN×GO

AN UNINVITED FRIEND OR FAMILY MEMBER RANDOMLY SHOWS UP.	SOMEONE KNOWS, AND SINGS, THE LYRICS TO EVERY SONG.	THERE'S A GARTER TOSS AND, YES, IT'S CREEPY.	A GIRL PUTS FOOD IN HER PURSE FOR LATER.	A GUEST TAKES THEIR THIRD TRIP TO THE BUFFET.
SOMEONE MAKES A DIRTY JOKE ABOUT THE COUPLE DURING THEIR SPEECH.	A DRUNK PERSON CONFESSES THEIR LOVE TO SOMEONE.	'I JUST LOVE WEDDINGS!'	SOMEONE HAS WAAAAAY TOO MUCH MAKEUP ON.	THE CAKE TOPPER INCLUDES A DOG.
SOMEONE TRIES TO BREAKDANCE & IT DOESN'T END WELL.	THE BRIDAL PARTY SCREAMS LIKE RAPTORS WHEN 'THEIR SONG' COMES ON.	✖	A POTENTIAL FIST FIGHT BECOMES AN ACTUAL FIST FIGHT.	AN ADULT IS SEATED AT THE KIDS TABLE PURELY OUT OF SPITE.
SOMEONE IS SITTING AT A TABLE COMPLETELY ALONE.	THE FIRST DANCE IS TO SOME JOHN LEGEND SONG.	A GUEST THINKS IT'S THE PERFECT MOMENT TO PROPOSE.	SOMEONE ANNOUNCES THEY'RE PREGNANT.	A SPEECH COMPLETELY OMITS ONE OF THE NEWLYWEDS.
MASON JARS ARE USED AS DECOR.	DISPOSABLE CAMERAS ARE LITERALLY EVERYWHERE.	THERE ARE CUPCAKES IN LIEU OF A WEDDING CAKE.	THE FOOD IS SERVED BUFFET STYLE—LIKE A FANCY GOLDEN CORRAL.	THERE'S A PHOTO BOOTH, COMPLETE W/ DEMEANING PROPS.

OBJECTIVE

OH, YOU MEAN BESIDES TRYING TO PASS THE TIME DURING THIS WEDDING THAT YOU MAY OR MAY NOT HAVE EVEN WANTED TO GO TO? ISN'T THAT ENOUGH? WHAT DO YOU WANT FROM US?

WELL, WE HOPE YOU'RE AT LEAST FAMILIAR WITH THE CONCEPT OF BINGO. BECAUSE IF NOT, WELL WE ARE REALLY KIND OF WORRIED ABOUT YOU. WHAT OTHER THINGS IN LIFE HAVE YOU MISSED? SHOES? AUTOMOBILES? TWO-PLY TOILET PAPER? WE DIGRESS.

THIS WEDDING BIN·GO GAME IS PLAYED MUCH LIKE THE TRADITIONAL ONE. YOUR GOAL IS TO SIMPLY BE THE FIRST TO FILL 5 SEQUENTIAL SQUARES IN A ROW, A COLUMN, OR EVEN DIAGONALLY (SEE FIGURE 1 BELOW).

FIGURE 1

SEE THAT X IN THE CENTER SQUARE OF YOUR BOARDS? THAT'S A FREE SQUARE—WHICH MEANS EVERY PLAYER GETS THIS ONE AUTOMATICALLY. IT REALLY HELPS SO...YOU'RE WELCOME

PLAYING THE GAME

AFTER DETERMINING HOW MANY PEOPLE ARE PLAYING, THE OWNER OF THE BOOK SHOULD PERF. OUT A CARD (OR TWO) FOR EVERYONE TO USE AS THEIR PLAY BOARD(S).

ALRIGHT, SO HERE'S HOW OUR GAME IS A BIT DIFFERENT. WE'VE PRE-FILLED EACH CARD WITH THE COMMON (YET RIDICULOUS) THINGS THAT ALWAYS SEEM TO HAPPEN AT THESE EVENTS. SO, INSTEAD OF SOMEONE JUST CALLING OUT NUMBERS, EVERYONE IS PEOPLE WATCHING INSTEAD. WHEN SOMETHING HAPPENS THAT IS ON ONE OF YOUR SQUARES, YOU CALL IT OUT* (AS DISCREETLY AS APPROPRIATE, OF COURSE) AND MARK OFF THE SQUARE. JUST MAKE SURE THE OTHER PLAYERS ARE AWARE.

BY THE WAY, BRIDES & GROOMS TEND TO DO UNIQUELY STUPID THINGS, SO WE PUT THEM IN. ATTENDING A SAME SEX MARRIAGE? AWESOME. FEEL FREE TO MODIFY THE SQUARES AS NEEDED.

WINNING

WHEN A PLAYER MARKS OFF A WINNING CARD, THEY SHOULD YELL* 'BINGO.' IN THE EVENT OF A TIE, THE FIRST TO SAY IT IS THE WINNER. EITHER WAY—EVERYONE ELSE IN THE ROOM WILL PROBABLY BE WONDERING WHAT THE HELL YOU ARE DOING. ADMITTEDLY IT MIGHT BE HARD TO MAKE A TRUE BINGO, SO YOU CAN ALSO DECIDE THAT THE PLAYER WITH THE MOST SQUARES MARKED OFF IS THE WINNER.

BONUS: YOU CAN ALSO PLAY THIS AS A DRINKING GAME. IT'S SIMPLE. WHEN SOMETHING HAPPENS ON YOUR CARD, YOU HAVE TO TAKE A DRINK. IF YOU MAKE A BINGO—WELL NOW EVERYONE ELSE HAS TO DRINK. JUST MAYBE WAIT UNTIL THE RECEPTION TO START DRINKING. THAT'S WHERE THE OPEN BAR IS ANYWAY.

*DON'T ACTUALLY YELL (OR TALK) DURING A WEDDING

THERE ARE LAWN GAMES INVOLVED.	A PAST RELATIONSHIP IS MENTIONED IN A SPEECH.	SOMEONE WHO IS TOO DRUNK TO MAKE A SPEECH MAKES A SPEECH.	A GUEST ALSO DECIDED TO WEAR A WHITE DRESS.	THIS THING IS CATERED BY A FOOD TRUCK.
A FORCED GROUP DANCE HAPPENS. THE MACARENA, ELECTRIC SLIDE, ETC.	IT'S A DRY WEDDING.	SOMEONE BROUGHT THEIR OWN BEER.	AN ENTIRE TABLE IS ON THEIR PHONES.	THERE ARE COCKTAILS THEMED AFTER THE COUPLE.
A BORED 5-YEAR-OLD JUST LAYS IN THE MIDDLE OF THE FLOOR.	A GUEST THINKS IT'S THE PERFECT MOMENT TO PROPOSE.	✖	2 HOURS IN & SOMEONE STILL HASN'T STOPPED CRYING.	THERE'S A GARTER TOSS AND, YES, IT'S CREEPY.
THERE ARE CUPCAKES IN LIEU OF A WEDDING CAKE.	SOMEONE GETS CAKE RELENTLESSLY SMASHED IN THEIR FACE.	THE FOOD IS SERVED BUFFET STYLE–LIKE A FANCY GOLDEN CORRAL.	SOMEONE HAS ON WAY TOO MUCH PERFUME/ COLOGNE.	SOMEONE SHOUT-SINGS ALONG TO EVERY SONG & NEVER KNOWS THE WORDS.
A GIRL PUTS FOOD IN HER PURSE FOR LATER.	THE BRIDE STARTS WALKING AROUND BAREFOOT.	SOMEONE WON'T STOP CHANTING 'KISS! KISS! KISS!' AT THE COUPLE.	AN OLDER GRANDPARENT AND/OR DRUNK UNCLE FALLS ASLEEP AT A TABLE.	THE FATHER DAUGHTER DANCE MUSIC IS A BIT TOO ROMANTIC.

OBJECTIVE

OH, YOU MEAN BESIDES TRYING TO PASS THE TIME DURING THIS WEDDING THAT YOU MAY OR MAY NOT HAVE EVEN WANTED TO GO TO? ISN'T THAT ENOUGH? WHAT DO YOU WANT FROM US?

WELL, WE HOPE YOU'RE AT LEAST FAMILIAR WITH THE CONCEPT OF BINGO. BECAUSE IF NOT, WELL WE ARE REALLY KIND OF WORRIED ABOUT YOU. WHAT OTHER THINGS IN LIFE HAVE YOU MISSED? SHOES? AUTOMOBILES? TWO-PLY TOILET PAPER? WE DIGRESS.

THIS WEDDING BIN×GO GAME IS PLAYED MUCH LIKE THE TRADITIONAL ONE. YOUR GOAL IS TO SIMPLY BE THE FIRST TO FILL 5 SEQUENTIAL SQUARES IN A ROW, A COLUMN, OR EVEN DIAGONALLY (SEE FIGURE 1 BELOW).

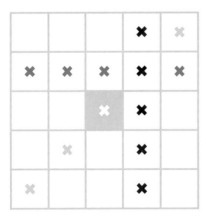

FIGURE 1

SEE THAT X IN THE CENTER SQUARE OF YOUR BOARDS? THAT'S A FREE SQUARE—WHICH MEANS EVERY PLAYER GETS THIS ONE AUTOMATICALLY. IT REALLY HELPS SO...YOU'RE WELCOME

PLAYING THE GAME

AFTER DETERMINING HOW MANY PEOPLE ARE PLAYING, THE OWNER OF THE BOOK SHOULD PERF. OUT A CARD (OR TWO) FOR EVERYONE TO USE AS THEIR PLAY BOARD(S).

ALRIGHT, SO HERE'S HOW OUR GAME IS A BIT DIFFERENT. WE'VE PRE-FILLED EACH CARD WITH THE COMMON (YET RIDICULOUS) THINGS THAT ALWAYS SEEM TO HAPPEN AT THESE EVENTS. SO, INSTEAD OF SOMEONE JUST CALLING OUT NUMBERS, EVERYONE IS PEOPLE WATCHING INSTEAD. WHEN SOMETHING HAPPENS THAT IS ON ONE OF YOUR SQUARES, YOU CALL IT OUT* (AS DISCREETLY AS APPROPRIATE, OF COURSE) AND MARK OFF THE SQUARE. JUST MAKE SURE THE OTHER PLAYERS ARE AWARE.

BY THE WAY, BRIDES & GROOMS TEND TO DO UNIQUELY STUPID THINGS, SO WE PUT THEM IN. ATTENDING A SAME SEX MARRIAGE? AWESOME. FEEL FREE TO MODIFY THE SQUARES AS NEEDED.

WINNING

WHEN A PLAYER MARKS OFF A WINNING CARD, THEY SHOULD YELL* 'BINGO.' IN THE EVENT OF A TIE, THE FIRST TO SAY IT IS THE WINNER. EITHER WAY—EVERYONE ELSE IN THE ROOM WILL PROBABLY BE WONDERING WHAT THE HELL YOU ARE DOING. ADMITTEDLY IT MIGHT BE HARD TO MAKE A TRUE BINGO, SO YOU CAN ALSO DECIDE THAT THE PLAYER WITH THE MOST SQUARES MARKED OFF IS THE WINNER.

BONUS: YOU CAN ALSO PLAY THIS AS A DRINKING GAME. IT'S SIMPLE. WHEN SOMETHING HAPPENS ON YOUR CARD, YOU HAVE TO TAKE A DRINK. IF YOU MAKE A BINGO—WELL NOW EVERYONE ELSE HAS TO DRINK. JUST MAYBE WAIT UNTIL THE RECEPTION TO START DRINKING. THAT'S WHERE THE OPEN BAR IS ANYWAY.

*DON'T ACTUALLY YELL (OR TALK) DURING A WEDDING.

BIN×GO

SOMEONE GETS CAKE RELENTLESSLY SMASHED IN THEIR FACE.	THIS THING IS CATERED BY A FOOD TRUCK.	THERE ARE COCKTAILS THEMED AFTER THE COUPLE.	SOMEONE HAS WAAAAAY TOO MUCH MAKEUP ON.	SOMEONE SHOUT-SINGS ALONG TO EVERY SONG & NEVER KNOWS THE WORDS.
THE CAKE TOPPER INCLUDES A DOG.	A DRUNK PERSON CONFESSES THEIR LOVE TO SOMEONE.	THE WEDDING DJ PRONOUNCES SOMEONE'S NAME WRONG.	'I JUST LOVE WEDDINGS!'	MASON JARS ARE USED AS DECOR.
'WOOOO!!' IS DRUNKENLY YELLED IN OTHERWISE SILENCE.	DRUNK BROS START PUNCHING EACH OTHER TO SHOW AFFECTION.	✖	2 HOURS IN & SOMEONE STILL HASN'T STOPPED CRYING.	A GUEST ALSO DECIDED TO WEAR A WHITE DRESS.
THE BRIDAL PARTY SCREAMS LIKE RAPTORS WHEN 'THEIR SONG' COMES ON.	SOMEONE ANNOUNCES THEY'RE PREGNANT.	THERE ARE LAWN GAMES INVOLVED.	A GIRL PUTS FOOD IN HER PURSE FOR LATER.	AN OLDER GRANDPARENT AND/OR DRUNK UNCLE FALLS ASLEEP AT A TABLE.
THERE'S A GARTER TOSS AND, YES, IT'S CREEPY.	SOMEONE TRIES TO BREAKDANCE & IT DOESN'T END WELL.	IT'S A DRY WEDDING.	A FORCED GROUP DANCE HAPPENS. THE MACARENA, ELECTRIC SLIDE, ETC.	A GIRL GETS BODY-CHECKED DURING THE BOUQUET TOSS.

OBJECTIVE

OH, YOU MEAN BESIDES TRYING TO PASS THE TIME DURING THIS WEDDING THAT YOU MAY OR MAY NOT HAVE EVEN WANTED TO GO TO? ISN'T THAT ENOUGH? WHAT DO YOU WANT FROM US?

WELL, WE HOPE YOU'RE AT LEAST FAMILIAR WITH THE CONCEPT OF BINGO. BECAUSE IF NOT, WELL WE ARE REALLY KIND OF WORRIED ABOUT YOU. WHAT OTHER THINGS IN LIFE HAVE YOU MISSED? SHOES? AUTOMOBILES? TWO-PLY TOILET PAPER? WE DIGRESS.

THIS WEDDING BIN·GO GAME IS PLAYED MUCH LIKE THE TRADITIONAL ONE. YOUR GOAL IS TO SIMPLY BE THE FIRST TO FILL 5 SEQUENTIAL SQUARES IN A ROW, A COLUMN, OR EVEN DIAGONALLY (SEE FIGURE 1 BELOW).

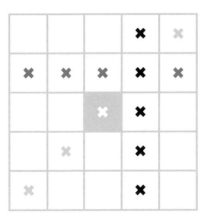

FIGURE 1

SEE THAT X IN THE CENTER SQUARE OF YOUR BOARDS? THAT'S A FREE SQUARE—WHICH MEANS EVERY PLAYER GETS THIS ONE AUTOMATICALLY. IT REALLY HELPS SO...YOU'RE WELCOME

PLAYING THE GAME

AFTER DETERMINING HOW MANY PEOPLE ARE PLAYING, THE OWNER OF THE BOOK SHOULD PERF. OUT A CARD (OR TWO) FOR EVERYONE TO USE AS THEIR PLAY BOARD(S).

ALRIGHT, SO HERE'S HOW OUR GAME IS A BIT DIFFERENT. WE'VE PRE-FILLED EACH CARD WITH THE COMMON (YET RIDICULOUS) THINGS THAT ALWAYS SEEM TO HAPPEN AT THESE EVENTS. SO, INSTEAD OF SOMEONE JUST CALLING OUT NUMBERS, EVERYONE IS PEOPLE WATCHING INSTEAD. WHEN SOMETHING HAPPENS THAT IS ON ONE OF YOUR SQUARES, YOU CALL IT OUT* (AS DISCREETLY AS APPROPRIATE, OF COURSE) AND MARK OFF THE SQUARE. JUST MAKE SURE THE OTHER PLAYERS ARE AWARE.

BY THE WAY, BRIDES & GROOMS TEND TO DO UNIQUELY STUPID THINGS, SO WE PUT THEM IN. ATTENDING A SAME SEX MARRIAGE? AWESOME. FEEL FREE TO MODIFY THE SQUARES AS NEEDED.

WINNING

WHEN A PLAYER MARKS OFF A WINNING CARD, THEY SHOULD YELL* 'BINGO.' IN THE EVENT OF A TIE, THE FIRST TO SAY IT IS THE WINNER. EITHER WAY—EVERYONE ELSE IN THE ROOM WILL PROBABLY BE WONDERING WHAT THE HELL YOU ARE DOING. ADMITTEDLY IT MIGHT BE HARD TO MAKE A TRUE BINGO, SO YOU CAN ALSO DECIDE THAT THE PLAYER WITH THE MOST SQUARES MARKED OFF IS THE WINNER.

BONUS: YOU CAN ALSO PLAY THIS AS A DRINKING GAME. IT'S SIMPLE. WHEN SOMETHING HAPPENS ON YOUR CARD, YOU HAVE TO TAKE A DRINK. IF YOU MAKE A BINGO—WELL NOW EVERYONE ELSE HAS TO DRINK. JUST MAYBE WAIT UNTIL THE RECEPTION TO START DRINKING. THAT'S WHERE THE OPEN BAR IS ANYWAY.

*DON'T ACTUALLY YELL (OR TALK) DURING A WEDDING.

A CHRONIC DANCER IS SWEATING PROFUSELY.	SOMEONE WON'T STOP CHANTING 'KISS! KISS! KISS!' AT THE COUPLE.	THE CAKE TOPPERS ARE DISNEY CHARACTERS.	ABSOLUTELY NO ONE KNOWS WHO ONE OF THE GUESTS IS.	A SPEECH COMPLETELY OMITS ONE OF THE NEWLYWEDS.
SOMEONE ANNOUNCES THEY'RE PREGNANT.	THERE'S A GARTER TOSS AND, YES, IT'S CREEPY.	AN OLDER GRANDPARENT AND/OR DRUNK UNCLE FALLS ASLEEP AT A TABLE.	THE FOOD IS SERVED BUFFET STYLE—LIKE A FANCY GOLDEN CORRAL.	A FORCED GROUP DANCE HAPPENS. THE MACARENA, ELECTRIC SLIDE, ETC.
A GUEST TAKES THEIR THIRD TRIP TO THE BUFFET.	THE BRIDAL PARTY SCREAMS LIKE RAPTORS WHEN 'THEIR SONG' COMES ON.	✖	A GIRL PUTS FOOD IN HER PURSE FOR LATER.	SOMEONE GETS CAKE RELENTLESSLY SMASHED IN THEIR FACE.
SOMEONE BROUGHT THEIR OWN BEER.	DRUNK BROS START PUNCHING EACH OTHER TO SHOW AFFECTION.	SOMEONE SHOUT-SINGS ALONG TO EVERY SONG & NEVER KNOWS THE WORDS.	THERE ARE COCKTAILS THEMED AFTER THE COUPLE.	A MEMBER OF THE WEDDING PARTY VOMITS.
SOMEONE TRIES TO BREAKDANCE & IT DOESN'T END WELL.	THE FATHER DAUGHTER DANCE MUSIC IS A BIT TOO ROMANTIC.	THE FIRST DANCE IS TO SOME JOHN LEGEND SONG.	SOMEONE HAS WAAAAAY TOO MUCH MAKEUP ON.	SOMEONE IS EATING AN UNGODLY AMOUNT OF CHEESE.

OBJECTIVE

OH, YOU MEAN BESIDES TRYING TO PASS THE TIME DURING THIS WEDDING THAT YOU MAY OR MAY NOT HAVE EVEN WANTED TO GO TO? ISN'T THAT ENOUGH? WHAT DO YOU WANT FROM US?

WELL, WE HOPE YOU'RE AT LEAST FAMILIAR WITH THE CONCEPT OF BINGO. BECAUSE IF NOT, WELL WE ARE REALLY KIND OF WORRIED ABOUT YOU. WHAT OTHER THINGS IN LIFE HAVE YOU MISSED? SHOES? AUTOMOBILES? TWO-PLY TOILET PAPER? WE DIGRESS.

THIS WEDDING BIN×GO GAME IS PLAYED MUCH LIKE THE TRADITIONAL ONE. YOUR GOAL IS TO SIMPLY BE THE FIRST TO FILL 5 SEQUENTIAL SQUARES IN A ROW, A COLUMN, OR EVEN DIAGONALLY (SEE FIGURE 1 BELOW).

FIGURE 1

SEE THAT X IN THE CENTER SQUARE OF YOUR BOARDS? THAT'S A FREE SQUARE—WHICH MEANS EVERY PLAYER GETS THIS ONE AUTOMATICALLY. IT REALLY HELPS SO...YOU'RE WELCOME

PLAYING THE GAME

AFTER DETERMINING HOW MANY PEOPLE ARE PLAYING, THE OWNER OF THE BOOK SHOULD PERF. OUT A CARD (OR TWO) FOR EVERYONE TO USE AS THEIR PLAY BOARD(S).

ALRIGHT, SO HERE'S HOW OUR GAME IS A BIT DIFFERENT. WE'VE PRE-FILLED EACH CARD WITH THE COMMON (YET RIDICULOUS) THINGS THAT ALWAYS SEEM TO HAPPEN AT THESE EVENTS. SO, INSTEAD OF SOMEONE JUST CALLING OUT NUMBERS, EVERYONE IS PEOPLE WATCHING INSTEAD. WHEN SOMETHING HAPPENS THAT IS ON ONE OF YOUR SQUARES, YOU CALL IT OUT* (AS DISCREETLY AS APPROPRIATE, OF COURSE) AND MARK OFF THE SQUARE. JUST MAKE SURE THE OTHER PLAYERS ARE AWARE.

BY THE WAY, BRIDES & GROOMS TEND TO DO UNIQUELY STUPID THINGS, SO WE PUT THEM IN. ATTENDING A SAME SEX MARRIAGE? AWESOME. FEEL FREE TO MODIFY THE SQUARES AS NEEDED.

WINNING

WHEN A PLAYER MARKS OFF A WINNING CARD, THEY SHOULD YELL* 'BINGO.' IN THE EVENT OF A TIE, THE FIRST TO SAY IT IS THE WINNER. EITHER WAY—EVERYONE ELSE IN THE ROOM WILL PROBABLY BE WONDERING WHAT THE HELL YOU ARE DOING. ADMITTEDLY IT MIGHT BE HARD TO MAKE A TRUE BINGO, SO YOU CAN ALSO DECIDE THAT THE PLAYER WITH THE MOST SQUARES MARKED OFF IS THE WINNER.

BONUS: YOU CAN ALSO PLAY THIS AS A DRINKING GAME. IT'S SIMPLE. WHEN SOMETHING HAPPENS ON YOUR CARD, YOU HAVE TO TAKE A DRINK. IF YOU MAKE A BINGO—WELL NOW EVERYONE ELSE HAS TO DRINK. JUST MAYBE WAIT UNTIL THE RECEPTION TO START DRINKING. THAT'S WHERE THE OPEN BAR IS ANYWAY.

*DON'T ACTUALLY YELL (OR TALK) DURING A WEDDING.

BIN×GO

A GUEST TAKES THEIR THIRD TRIP TO THE BUFFET.	ABSOLUTELY NO ONE KNOWS WHO ONE OF THE GUESTS IS.	A CHRONIC DANCER IS SWEATING PROFUSELY.	DISPOSABLE CAMERAS ARE LITERALLY EVERYWHERE.	SOMEONE IS EATING AN UNGODLY AMOUNT OF CHEESE.
A PAST RELATIONSHIP IS MENTIONED IN A SPEECH.	THERE ARE LAWN GAMES INVOLVED.	THERE'S A PHOTO BOOTH, COMPLETE W/ DEMEANING PROPS.	'I JUST LOVE WEDDINGS!'	'WOOOO!!' IS DRUNKENLY YELLED IN OTHERWISE SILENCE.
AN ADULT IS SEATED AT THE KIDS TABLE PURELY OUT OF SPITE.	THE FIRST DANCE IS TO SOME JOHN LEGEND SONG.	✖	'I REMEMBER THE NIGHT YOU MET' IS SAID DURING A SPEECH.	SOMEONE BROUGHT THEIR OWN BEER.
SOMEONE SHOUT-SINGS ALONG TO EVERY SONG & NEVER KNOWS THE WORDS.	SOMEONE IS SITTING AT A TABLE COMPLETELY ALONE.	A GIRL GETS BODY-CHECKED DURING THE BOUQUET TOSS.	AN OLDER GRANDPARENT AND/OR DRUNK UNCLE FALLS ASLEEP AT A TABLE.	THE FOOD IS SERVED BUFFET STYLE—LIKE A FANCY GOLDEN CORRAL.
THE WEDDING DJ PRONOUNCES SOMEONE'S NAME WRONG.	SOMEONE GETS CAKE RELENTLESSLY SMASHED IN THEIR FACE.	SOMEONE HAS ON WAY TOO MUCH PERFUME/ COLOGNE.	MASON JARS ARE USED AS DECOR.	THE BRIDAL PARTY SCREAMS LIKE RAPTORS WHEN 'THEIR SONG' COMES ON.

OBJECTIVE

OH, YOU MEAN BESIDES TRYING TO PASS THE TIME DURING THIS WEDDING THAT YOU MAY OR MAY NOT HAVE EVEN WANTED TO GO TO? ISN'T THAT ENOUGH? WHAT DO YOU WANT FROM US?

WELL, WE HOPE YOU'RE AT LEAST FAMILIAR WITH THE CONCEPT OF BINGO. BECAUSE IF NOT, WELL WE ARE REALLY KIND OF WORRIED ABOUT YOU. WHAT OTHER THINGS IN LIFE HAVE YOU MISSED? SHOES? AUTOMOBILES? TWO-PLY TOILET PAPER? WE DIGRESS.

THIS WEDDING BIN⋅GO GAME IS PLAYED MUCH LIKE THE TRADITIONAL ONE. YOUR GOAL IS TO SIMPLY BE THE FIRST TO FILL 5 SEQUENTIAL SQUARES IN A ROW, A COLUMN, OR EVEN DIAGONALLY (SEE FIGURE 1 BELOW).

FIGURE 1

SEE THAT X IN THE CENTER SQUARE OF YOUR BOARDS? THAT'S A FREE SQUARE—WHICH MEANS EVERY PLAYER GETS THIS ONE AUTOMATICALLY. IT REALLY HELPS SO...YOU'RE WELCOME

PLAYING THE GAME

AFTER DETERMINING HOW MANY PEOPLE ARE PLAYING, THE OWNER OF THE BOOK SHOULD PERF. OUT A CARD (OR TWO) FOR EVERYONE TO USE AS THEIR PLAY BOARD(S).

ALRIGHT, SO HERE'S HOW OUR GAME IS A BIT DIFFERENT. WE'VE PRE-FILLED EACH CARD WITH THE COMMON (YET RIDICULOUS) THINGS THAT ALWAYS SEEM TO HAPPEN AT THESE EVENTS. SO, INSTEAD OF SOMEONE JUST CALLING OUT NUMBERS, EVERYONE IS PEOPLE WATCHING INSTEAD. WHEN SOMETHING HAPPENS THAT IS ON ONE OF YOUR SQUARES, YOU CALL IT OUT* (AS DISCREETLY AS APPROPRIATE, OF COURSE) AND MARK OFF THE SQUARE. JUST MAKE SURE THE OTHER PLAYERS ARE AWARE.

BY THE WAY, BRIDES & GROOMS TEND TO DO UNIQUELY STUPID THINGS, SO WE PUT THEM IN. ATTENDING A SAME SEX MARRIAGE? AWESOME. FEEL FREE TO MODIFY THE SQUARES AS NEEDED.

WINNING

WHEN A PLAYER MARKS OFF A WINNING CARD, THEY SHOULD YELL* 'BINGO.' IN THE EVENT OF A TIE, THE FIRST TO SAY IT IS THE WINNER. EITHER WAY—EVERYONE ELSE IN THE ROOM WILL PROBABLY BE WONDERING WHAT THE HELL YOU ARE DOING. ADMITTEDLY IT MIGHT BE HARD TO MAKE A TRUE BINGO, SO YOU CAN ALSO DECIDE THAT THE PLAYER WITH THE MOST SQUARES MARKED OFF IS THE WINNER.

BONUS: YOU CAN ALSO PLAY THIS AS A DRINKING GAME. IT'S SIMPLE. WHEN SOMETHING HAPPENS ON YOUR CARD, YOU HAVE TO TAKE A DRINK. IF YOU MAKE A BINGO—WELL NOW EVERYONE ELSE HAS TO DRINK. JUST MAYBE WAIT UNTIL THE RECEPTION TO START DRINKING. THAT'S WHERE THE OPEN BAR IS ANYWAY.

*DON'T ACTUALLY YELL (OR TALK) DURING A WEDDING

AN OLDER COUPLE STARTS DIRTY DANCING TO A MODERN SONG.	DISPOSABLE CAMERAS ARE LITERALLY EVERYWHERE.	THE BRIDE STARTS WALKING AROUND BAREFOOT.	SOMEONE WHO IS TOO DRUNK TO MAKE A SPEECH MAKES A SPEECH.	A FORCED GROUP DANCE HAPPENS. THE MACARENA, ELECTRIC SLIDE, ETC.
A BORED 5-YEAR-OLD JUST LAYS IN THE MIDDLE OF THE FLOOR.	THE FIRST DANCE IS TO SOME JOHN LEGEND SONG.	SOMEONE MAKES A DIRTY JOKE ABOUT THE COUPLE DURING THEIR SPEECH.	THERE ARE CUPCAKES IN LIEU OF A WEDDING CAKE.	A GUEST THINKS IT'S THE PERFECT MOMENT TO PROPOSE.
THE FOOD IS SERVED BUFFET STYLE—LIKE A FANCY GOLDEN CORRAL.	SOMEONE KNOWS, AND SINGS, THE LYRICS TO EVERY SONG.	✖	AN UNINVITED FRIEND OR FAMILY MEMBER RANDOMLY SHOWS UP.	A DISTANT RELATIVE CLOSE-TALKS WITH THE COUPLE FOR 30 MINUTES.
SOMEONE SHOUT-SINGS ALONG TO EVERY SONG & NEVER KNOWS THE WORDS.	SOMEONE GETS CAKE RELENTLESSLY SMASHED IN THEIR FACE.	A GUEST TAKES THEIR THIRD TRIP TO THE BUFFET.	AN ADULT IS SEATED AT THE KIDS TABLE PURELY OUT OF SPITE.	THERE ARE COCKTAILS THEMED AFTER THE COUPLE.
A POTENTIAL FIST FIGHT BECOMES AN ACTUAL FIST FIGHT.	THE COUPLE IS INTRODUCED TO THE THEME OF 'ROCKY' OR SOME CRAP.	THERE'S A PHOTO BOOTH, COMPLETE W/ DEMEANING PROPS.	'SO, HOW LONG DO YOU THINK THIS ONE WILL LAST?'	AN OLDER GRANDPARENT AND/OR DRUNK UNCLE FALLS ASLEEP AT A TABLE.

OBJECTIVE

OH, YOU MEAN BESIDES TRYING TO PASS THE TIME DURING THIS WEDDING THAT YOU MAY OR MAY NOT HAVE EVEN WANTED TO GO TO? ISN'T THAT ENOUGH? WHAT DO YOU WANT FROM US?

WELL, WE HOPE YOU'RE AT LEAST FAMILIAR WITH THE CONCEPT OF BINGO. BECAUSE IF NOT, WELL WE ARE REALLY KIND OF WORRIED ABOUT YOU. WHAT OTHER THINGS IN LIFE HAVE YOU MISSED? SHOES? AUTOMOBILES? TWO-PLY TOILET PAPER? WE DIGRESS.

THIS WEDDING BIN·GO GAME IS PLAYED MUCH LIKE THE TRADITIONAL ONE. YOUR GOAL IS TO SIMPLY BE THE FIRST TO FILL 5 SEQUENTIAL SQUARES IN A ROW, A COLUMN, OR EVEN DIAGONALLY (SEE FIGURE 1 BELOW).

FIGURE 1

SEE THAT X IN THE CENTER SQUARE OF YOUR BOARDS? THAT'S A FREE SQUARE—WHICH MEANS EVERY PLAYER GETS THIS ONE AUTOMATICALLY. IT REALLY HELPS SO...YOU'RE WELCOME

PLAYING THE GAME

AFTER DETERMINING HOW MANY PEOPLE ARE PLAYING, THE OWNER OF THE BOOK SHOULD PERF. OUT A CARD (OR TWO) FOR EVERYONE TO USE AS THEIR PLAY BOARD(S).

ALRIGHT, SO HERE'S HOW OUR GAME IS A BIT DIFFERENT. WE'VE PRE-FILLED EACH CARD WITH THE COMMON (YET RIDICULOUS) THINGS THAT ALWAYS SEEM TO HAPPEN AT THESE EVENTS. SO, INSTEAD OF SOMEONE JUST CALLING OUT NUMBERS, EVERYONE IS PEOPLE WATCHING INSTEAD. WHEN SOMETHING HAPPENS THAT IS ON ONE OF YOUR SQUARES, YOU CALL IT OUT* (AS DISCREETLY AS APPROPRIATE, OF COURSE) AND MARK OFF THE SQUARE. JUST MAKE SURE THE OTHER PLAYERS ARE AWARE.

BY THE WAY, BRIDES & GROOMS TEND TO DO UNIQUELY STUPID THINGS, SO WE PUT THEM IN. ATTENDING A SAME SEX MARRIAGE? AWESOME. FEEL FREE TO MODIFY THE SQUARES AS NEEDED.

WINNING

WHEN A PLAYER MARKS OFF A WINNING CARD, THEY SHOULD YELL* 'BINGO.' IN THE EVENT OF A TIE, THE FIRST TO SAY IT IS THE WINNER. EITHER WAY—EVERYONE ELSE IN THE ROOM WILL PROBABLY BE WONDERING WHAT THE HELL YOU ARE DOING. ADMITTEDLY IT MIGHT BE HARD TO MAKE A TRUE BINGO, SO YOU CAN ALSO DECIDE THAT THE PLAYER WITH THE MOST SQUARES MARKED OFF IS THE WINNER.

BONUS: YOU CAN ALSO PLAY THIS AS A DRINKING GAME. IT'S SIMPLE. WHEN SOMETHING HAPPENS ON YOUR CARD, YOU HAVE TO TAKE A DRINK. IF YOU MAKE A BINGO—WELL NOW EVERYONE ELSE HAS TO DRINK. JUST MAYBE WAIT UNTIL THE RECEPTION TO START DRINKING. THAT'S WHERE THE OPEN BAR IS ANYWAY.

*DON'T ACTUALLY YELL (OR TALK) DURING A WEDDING

RECEPTION BIN×GO RECEPTION

A GUEST THINKS IT'S THE PERFECT MOMENT TO PROPOSE.	AN ENTIRE TABLE IS ON THEIR PHONES.	'WOOOO!!' IS DRUNKENLY YELLED IN OTHERWISE SILENCE.	AN OLDER COUPLE STARTS DIRTY DANCING TO A MODERN SONG.	SOMEONE TRIES TO BREAKDANCE & IT DOESN'T END WELL.
A DRUNK PERSON CONFESSES THEIR LOVE TO SOMEONE.	DRUNK BROS START PUNCHING EACH OTHER TO SHOW AFFECTION.	2 HOURS IN & SOMEONE STILL HASN'T STOPPED CRYING.	AN ADULT IS SEATED AT THE KIDS TABLE PURELY OUT OF SPITE.	A PAST RELATIONSHIP IS MENTIONED IN A SPEECH.
AN UNINVITED FRIEND OR FAMILY MEMBER RANDOMLY SHOWS UP.	A GUEST ALSO DECIDED TO WEAR A WHITE DRESS.	✖	MASON JARS ARE USED AS DECOR.	THE BRIDAL PARTY SCREAMS LIKE RAPTORS WHEN 'THEIR SONG' COMES ON.
ABSOLUTELY NO ONE KNOWS WHO ONE OF THE GUESTS IS.	'I REMEMBER THE NIGHT YOU MET' IS SAID DURING A SPEECH.	THIS THING IS CATERED BY A FOOD TRUCK.	A FORCED GROUP DANCE HAPPENS. THE MACARENA, ELECTRIC SLIDE, ETC.	SOMEONE HAS WAAAAAY TOO MUCH MAKEUP ON.
THE CAKE TOPPERS ARE DISNEY CHARACTERS.	THE FATHER DAUGHTER DANCE MUSIC IS A BIT TOO ROMANTIC.	THERE'S A GARTER TOSS AND, YES, IT'S CREEPY.	A GIRL PUTS FOOD IN HER PURSE FOR LATER.	SOMEONE KNOWS, AND SINGS, THE LYRICS TO EVERY SONG.

OBJECTIVE

OH, YOU MEAN BESIDES TRYING TO PASS THE TIME DURING THIS WEDDING THAT YOU MAY OR MAY NOT HAVE EVEN WANTED TO GO TO? ISN'T THAT ENOUGH? WHAT DO YOU WANT FROM US?

WELL, WE HOPE YOU'RE AT LEAST FAMILIAR WITH THE CONCEPT OF BINGO. BECAUSE IF NOT, WELL WE ARE REALLY KIND OF WORRIED ABOUT YOU. WHAT OTHER THINGS IN LIFE HAVE YOU MISSED? SHOES? AUTOMOBILES? TWO-PLY TOILET PAPER? WE DIGRESS.

THIS WEDDING BIN·GO GAME IS PLAYED MUCH LIKE THE TRADITIONAL ONE. YOUR GOAL IS TO SIMPLY BE THE FIRST TO FILL 5 SEQUENTIAL SQUARES IN A ROW, A COLUMN, OR EVEN DIAGONALLY (SEE FIGURE 1 BELOW).

FIGURE 1

SEE THAT X IN THE CENTER SQUARE OF YOUR BOARDS? THAT'S A FREE SQUARE—WHICH MEANS EVERY PLAYER GETS THIS ONE AUTOMATICALLY. IT REALLY HELPS SO...YOU'RE WELCOME

PLAYING THE GAME

AFTER DETERMINING HOW MANY PEOPLE ARE PLAYING, THE OWNER OF THE BOOK SHOULD PERF. OUT A CARD (OR TWO) FOR EVERYONE TO USE AS THEIR PLAY BOARD(S).

ALRIGHT, SO HERE'S HOW OUR GAME IS A BIT DIFFERENT. WE'VE PRE-FILLED EACH CARD WITH THE COMMON (YET RIDICULOUS) THINGS THAT ALWAYS SEEM TO HAPPEN AT THESE EVENTS. SO, INSTEAD OF SOMEONE JUST CALLING OUT NUMBERS, EVERYONE IS PEOPLE WATCHING INSTEAD. WHEN SOMETHING HAPPENS THAT IS ON ONE OF YOUR SQUARES, YOU CALL IT OUT* (AS DISCREETLY AS APPROPRIATE, OF COURSE) AND MARK OFF THE SQUARE. JUST MAKE SURE THE OTHER PLAYERS ARE AWARE.

BY THE WAY, BRIDES & GROOMS TEND TO DO UNIQUELY STUPID THINGS, SO WE PUT THEM IN. ATTENDING A SAME SEX MARRIAGE? AWESOME. FEEL FREE TO MODIFY THE SQUARES AS NEEDED.

WINNING

WHEN A PLAYER MARKS OFF A WINNING CARD, THEY SHOULD YELL* 'BINGO.' IN THE EVENT OF A TIE, THE FIRST TO SAY IT IS THE WINNER. EITHER WAY—EVERYONE ELSE IN THE ROOM WILL PROBABLY BE WONDERING WHAT THE HELL YOU ARE DOING. ADMITTEDLY IT MIGHT BE HARD TO MAKE A TRUE BINGO, SO YOU CAN ALSO DECIDE THAT THE PLAYER WITH THE MOST SQUARES MARKED OFF IS THE WINNER.

BONUS: YOU CAN ALSO PLAY THIS AS A DRINKING GAME. IT'S SIMPLE. WHEN SOMETHING HAPPENS ON YOUR CARD, YOU HAVE TO TAKE A DRINK. IF YOU MAKE A BINGO—WELL NOW EVERYONE ELSE HAS TO DRINK. JUST MAYBE WAIT UNTIL THE RECEPTION TO START DRINKING. THAT'S WHERE THE OPEN BAR IS ANYWAY.

*DON'T ACTUALLY YELL (OR TALK) DURING A WEDDING.

BIN×GO

A MEMBER OF THE WEDDING PARTY VOMITS.	IT'S A DRY WEDDING.	DISPOSABLE CAMERAS ARE LITERALLY EVERYWHERE.	DRUNK BROS START PUNCHING EACH OTHER TO SHOW AFFECTION.	'I JUST LOVE WEDDINGS!'
THE CAKE TOPPER INCLUDES A DOG.	SOMEONE ANNOUNCES THEY'RE PREGNANT.	SOMEONE BROUGHT THEIR OWN BEER.	A GUEST TAKES THEIR THIRD TRIP TO THE BUFFET.	THE COUPLE IS INTRODUCED TO THE THEME OF 'ROCKY' OR SOME CRAP.
A POTENTIAL FIST FIGHT ENDS IN AGGRESSIVE HUGGING.	AN ADULT IS SEATED AT THE KIDS TABLE PURELY OUT OF SPITE.	✖	THERE'S A GARTER TOSS AND, YES, IT'S CREEPY.	THE FATHER DAUGHTER DANCE MUSIC IS A BIT TOO ROMANTIC.
THE BRIDE STARTS WALKING AROUND BAREFOOT.	SOMEONE IS SITTING AT A TABLE COMPLETELY ALONE.	'SO, HOW LONG DO YOU THINK THIS ONE WILL LAST?'	A CHRONIC DANCER IS SWEATING PROFUSELY.	A GIRL PUTS FOOD IN HER PURSE FOR LATER.
A GIRL GETS BODY-CHECKED DURING THE BOUQUET TOSS.	SOMEONE WON'T STOP CHANTING 'KISS! KISS! KISS!' AT THE COUPLE.	SOMEONE HAS ON WAY TOO MUCH PERFUME/ COLOGNE.	AN UNINVITED FRIEND OR FAMILY MEMBER RANDOMLY SHOWS UP.	2 HOURS IN & SOMEONE STILL HASN'T STOPPED CRYING.

OBJECTIVE

OH, YOU MEAN BESIDES TRYING TO PASS THE TIME DURING THIS WEDDING THAT YOU MAY OR MAY NOT HAVE EVEN WANTED TO GO TO? ISN'T THAT ENOUGH? WHAT DO YOU WANT FROM US?

WELL, WE HOPE YOU'RE AT LEAST FAMILIAR WITH THE CONCEPT OF BINGO. BECAUSE IF NOT, WELL WE ARE REALLY KIND OF WORRIED ABOUT YOU. WHAT OTHER THINGS IN LIFE HAVE YOU MISSED? SHOES? AUTOMOBILES? TWO-PLY TOILET PAPER? WE DIGRESS.

THIS WEDDING BIN·GO GAME IS PLAYED MUCH LIKE THE TRADITIONAL ONE. YOUR GOAL IS TO SIMPLY BE THE FIRST TO FILL 5 SEQUENTIAL SQUARES IN A ROW, A COLUMN, OR EVEN DIAGONALLY (SEE FIGURE 1 BELOW).

FIGURE 1

SEE THAT X IN THE CENTER SQUARE OF YOUR BOARDS? THAT'S A FREE SQUARE—WHICH MEANS EVERY PLAYER GETS THIS ONE AUTOMATICALLY. IT REALLY HELPS SO...YOU'RE WELCOME

PLAYING THE GAME

AFTER DETERMINING HOW MANY PEOPLE ARE PLAYING, THE OWNER OF THE BOOK SHOULD PERF. OUT A CARD (OR TWO) FOR EVERYONE TO USE AS THEIR PLAY BOARD(S).

ALRIGHT, SO HERE'S HOW OUR GAME IS A BIT DIFFERENT. WE'VE PRE-FILLED EACH CARD WITH THE COMMON (YET RIDICULOUS) THINGS THAT ALWAYS SEEM TO HAPPEN AT THESE EVENTS. SO, INSTEAD OF SOMEONE JUST CALLING OUT NUMBERS, EVERYONE IS PEOPLE WATCHING INSTEAD. WHEN SOMETHING HAPPENS THAT IS ON ONE OF YOUR SQUARES, YOU CALL IT OUT* (AS DISCREETLY AS APPROPRIATE, OF COURSE) AND MARK OFF THE SQUARE. JUST MAKE SURE THE OTHER PLAYERS ARE AWARE.

BY THE WAY, BRIDES & GROOMS TEND TO DO UNIQUELY STUPID THINGS, SO WE PUT THEM IN. ATTENDING A SAME SEX MARRIAGE? AWESOME. FEEL FREE TO MODIFY THE SQUARES AS NEEDED.

WINNING

WHEN A PLAYER MARKS OFF A WINNING CARD, THEY SHOULD YELL* 'BINGO.' IN THE EVENT OF A TIE, THE FIRST TO SAY IT IS THE WINNER. EITHER WAY—EVERYONE ELSE IN THE ROOM WILL PROBABLY BE WONDERING WHAT THE HELL YOU ARE DOING. ADMITTEDLY IT MIGHT BE HARD TO MAKE A TRUE BINGO, SO YOU CAN ALSO DECIDE THAT THE PLAYER WITH THE MOST SQUARES MARKED OFF IS THE WINNER.

BONUS: YOU CAN ALSO PLAY THIS AS A DRINKING GAME. IT'S SIMPLE. WHEN SOMETHING HAPPENS ON YOUR CARD, YOU HAVE TO TAKE A DRINK. IF YOU MAKE A BINGO—WELL NOW EVERYONE ELSE HAS TO DRINK. JUST MAYBE WAIT UNTIL THE RECEPTION TO START DRINKING. THAT'S WHERE THE OPEN BAR IS ANYWAY.

*DON'T ACTUALLY YELL (OR TALK) DURING A WEDDING.

BIN×GO

SOMEONE ANNOUNCES THEY'RE PREGNANT.	A GUEST ALSO DECIDED TO WEAR A WHITE DRESS.	A BORED 5-YEAR-OLD JUST LAYS IN THE MIDDLE OF THE FLOOR.	THE BRIDE STARTS WALKING AROUND BAREFOOT.	THE CAKE TOPPERS ARE DISNEY CHARACTERS.
SOMEONE IS EATING AN UNGODLY AMOUNT OF CHEESE.	IT'S A DRY WEDDING.	THE CAKE TOPPER INCLUDES A DOG.	SOMEONE MAKES A DIRTY JOKE ABOUT THE COUPLE DURING THEIR SPEECH.	AN UNINVITED FRIEND OR FAMILY MEMBER RANDOMLY SHOWS UP.
SOMEONE SHOUT-SINGS ALONG TO EVERY SONG & NEVER KNOWS THE WORDS.	A FORCED GROUP DANCE HAPPENS. THE MACARENA, ELECTRIC SLIDE, ETC.	✖	AN OLDER GRANDPARENT AND/OR DRUNK UNCLE FALLS ASLEEP AT A TABLE.	THE BRIDAL PARTY SCREAMS LIKE RAPTORS WHEN 'THEIR SONG' COMES ON.
THERE'S A GARTER TOSS AND, YES, IT'S CREEPY.	THE FATHER DAUGHTER DANCE MUSIC IS A BIT TOO ROMANTIC.	SOMEONE HAS WAAAAAY TOO MUCH MAKEUP ON.	ABSOLUTELY NO ONE KNOWS WHO ONE OF THE GUESTS IS.	THE WEDDING DJ PRONOUNCES SOMEONE'S NAME WRONG.
A GUEST THINKS IT'S THE PERFECT MOMENT TO PROPOSE.	A POTENTIAL FIST FIGHT BECOMES AN ACTUAL FIST FIGHT.	SOMEONE TRIES TO BREAKDANCE & IT DOESN'T END WELL.	SOMEONE IS SITTING AT A TABLE COMPLETELY ALONE.	A SPEECH COMPLETELY OMITS ONE OF THE NEWLYWEDS.

BIN×GO

OBJECTIVE

OH, YOU MEAN BESIDES TRYING TO PASS THE TIME DURING THIS WEDDING THAT YOU MAY OR MAY NOT HAVE EVEN WANTED TO GO TO? ISN'T THAT ENOUGH? WHAT DO YOU WANT FROM US?

WELL, WE HOPE YOU'RE AT LEAST FAMILIAR WITH THE CONCEPT OF BINGO. BECAUSE IF NOT, WELL WE ARE REALLY KIND OF WORRIED ABOUT YOU. WHAT OTHER THINGS IN LIFE HAVE YOU MISSED? SHOES? AUTOMOBILES? TWO-PLY TOILET PAPER? WE DIGRESS.

THIS WEDDING BIN·GO GAME IS PLAYED MUCH LIKE THE TRADITIONAL ONE. YOUR GOAL IS TO SIMPLY BE THE FIRST TO FILL 5 SEQUENTIAL SQUARES IN A ROW, A COLUMN, OR EVEN DIAGONALLY (SEE FIGURE 1 BELOW).

FIGURE 1

SEE THAT X IN THE CENTER SQUARE OF YOUR BOARDS? THAT'S A FREE SQUARE—WHICH MEANS EVERY PLAYER GETS THIS ONE AUTOMATICALLY. IT REALLY HELPS SO...YOU'RE WELCOME

PLAYING THE GAME

AFTER DETERMINING HOW MANY PEOPLE ARE PLAYING, THE OWNER OF THE BOOK SHOULD PERF. OUT A CARD (OR TWO) FOR EVERYONE TO USE AS THEIR PLAY BOARD(S).

ALRIGHT, SO HERE'S HOW OUR GAME IS A BIT DIFFERENT. WE'VE PRE-FILLED EACH CARD WITH THE COMMON (YET RIDICULOUS) THINGS THAT ALWAYS SEEM TO HAPPEN AT THESE EVENTS. SO, INSTEAD OF SOMEONE JUST CALLING OUT NUMBERS, EVERYONE IS PEOPLE WATCHING INSTEAD. WHEN SOMETHING HAPPENS THAT IS ON ONE OF YOUR SQUARES, YOU CALL IT OUT* (AS DISCREETLY AS APPROPRIATE, OF COURSE) AND MARK OFF THE SQUARE. JUST MAKE SURE THE OTHER PLAYERS ARE AWARE.

BY THE WAY, BRIDES & GROOMS TEND TO DO UNIQUELY STUPID THINGS, SO WE PUT THEM IN. ATTENDING A SAME SEX MARRIAGE? AWESOME. FEEL FREE TO MODIFY THE SQUARES AS NEEDED.

WINNING

WHEN A PLAYER MARKS OFF A WINNING CARD, THEY SHOULD YELL* 'BINGO.' IN THE EVENT OF A TIE, THE FIRST TO SAY IT IS THE WINNER. EITHER WAY—EVERYONE ELSE IN THE ROOM WILL PROBABLY BE WONDERING WHAT THE HELL YOU ARE DOING. ADMITTEDLY IT MIGHT BE HARD TO MAKE A TRUE BINGO, SO YOU CAN ALSO DECIDE THAT THE PLAYER WITH THE MOST SQUARES MARKED OFF IS THE WINNER.

BONUS: YOU CAN ALSO PLAY THIS AS A DRINKING GAME. IT'S SIMPLE. WHEN SOMETHING HAPPENS ON YOUR CARD, YOU HAVE TO TAKE A DRINK. IF YOU MAKE A BINGO—WELL NOW EVERYONE ELSE HAS TO DRINK. JUST MAYBE WAIT UNTIL THE RECEPTION TO START DRINKING. THAT'S WHERE THE OPEN BAR IS ANYWAY.

*DON'T ACTUALLY YELL (OR TALK) DURING A WEDDING.

BIN×GO

A MEMBER OF THE WEDDING PARTY VOMITS.	SOMEONE BROUGHT THEIR OWN BEER.	SOMEONE IS EATING AN UNGODLY AMOUNT OF CHEESE.	SOMEONE IS SITTING AT A TABLE COMPLETELY ALONE.	SOMEONE HAS WAAAAAY TOO MUCH MAKEUP ON.
'I JUST LOVE WEDDINGS!'	A GIRL PUTS FOOD IN HER PURSE FOR LATER.	SOMEONE TRIES TO BREAKDANCE & IT DOESN'T END WELL.	SOMEONE ANNOUNCES THEY'RE PREGNANT.	AN ADULT IS SEATED AT THE KIDS TABLE PURELY OUT OF SPITE.
A DRUNK PERSON CONFESSES THEIR LOVE TO SOMEONE.	THE FATHER DAUGHTER DANCE MUSIC IS A BIT TOO ROMANTIC.	✖	THERE ARE CUPCAKES IN LIEU OF A WEDDING CAKE.	'WOOOO!!' IS DRUNKENLY YELLED IN OTHERWISE SILENCE.
THE BRIDAL PARTY SCREAMS LIKE RAPTORS WHEN 'THEIR SONG' COMES ON.	A GIRL GETS BODY-CHECKED DURING THE BOUQUET TOSS.	MASON JARS ARE USED AS DECOR.	SOMEONE HAS ON WAY TOO MUCH PERFUME/ COLOGNE.	THERE ARE COCKTAILS THEMED AFTER THE COUPLE.
AN UNINVITED FRIEND OR FAMILY MEMBER RANDOMLY SHOWS UP.	DRUNK BROS START PUNCHING EACH OTHER TO SHOW AFFECTION.	SOMEONE MAKES A DIRTY JOKE ABOUT THE COUPLE DURING THEIR SPEECH.	THERE ARE LAWN GAMES INVOLVED.	SOMEONE GETS CAKE RELENTLESSLY SMASHED IN THEIR FACE.

OBJECTIVE

OH, YOU MEAN BESIDES TRYING TO PASS THE TIME DURING THIS WEDDING THAT YOU MAY OR MAY NOT HAVE EVEN WANTED TO GO TO? ISN'T THAT ENOUGH? WHAT DO YOU WANT FROM US?

WELL, WE HOPE YOU'RE AT LEAST FAMILIAR WITH THE CONCEPT OF BINGO. BECAUSE IF NOT, WELL WE ARE REALLY KIND OF WORRIED ABOUT YOU. WHAT OTHER THINGS IN LIFE HAVE YOU MISSED? SHOES? AUTOMOBILES? TWO-PLY TOILET PAPER? WE DIGRESS.

THIS WEDDING BIN×GO GAME IS PLAYED MUCH LIKE THE TRADITIONAL ONE. YOUR GOAL IS TO SIMPLY BE THE FIRST TO FILL 5 SEQUENTIAL SQUARES IN A ROW, A COLUMN, OR EVEN DIAGONALLY (SEE FIGURE 1 BELOW).

FIGURE 1

SEE THAT X IN THE CENTER SQUARE OF YOUR BOARDS? THAT'S A FREE SQUARE—WHICH MEANS EVERY PLAYER GETS THIS ONE AUTOMATICALLY. IT REALLY HELPS SO...YOU'RE WELCOME

PLAYING THE GAME

AFTER DETERMINING HOW MANY PEOPLE ARE PLAYING, THE OWNER OF THE BOOK SHOULD PERF. OUT A CARD (OR TWO) FOR EVERYONE TO USE AS THEIR PLAY BOARD(S).

ALRIGHT, SO HERE'S HOW OUR GAME IS A BIT DIFFERENT. WE'VE PRE-FILLED EACH CARD WITH THE COMMON (YET RIDICULOUS) THINGS THAT ALWAYS SEEM TO HAPPEN AT THESE EVENTS. SO, INSTEAD OF SOMEONE JUST CALLING OUT NUMBERS, EVERYONE IS PEOPLE WATCHING INSTEAD. WHEN SOMETHING HAPPENS THAT IS ON ONE OF YOUR SQUARES, YOU CALL IT OUT* (AS DISCREETLY AS APPROPRIATE, OF COURSE) AND MARK OFF THE SQUARE. JUST MAKE SURE THE OTHER PLAYERS ARE AWARE.

BY THE WAY, BRIDES & GROOMS TEND TO DO UNIQUELY STUPID THINGS, SO WE PUT THEM IN. ATTENDING A SAME SEX MARRIAGE? AWESOME. FEEL FREE TO MODIFY THE SQUARES AS NEEDED.

WINNING

WHEN A PLAYER MARKS OFF A WINNING CARD, THEY SHOULD YELL* 'BINGO.' IN THE EVENT OF A TIE, THE FIRST TO SAY IT IS THE WINNER. EITHER WAY—EVERYONE ELSE IN THE ROOM WILL PROBABLY BE WONDERING WHAT THE HELL YOU ARE DOING. ADMITTEDLY IT MIGHT BE HARD TO MAKE A TRUE BINGO, SO YOU CAN ALSO DECIDE THAT THE PLAYER WITH THE MOST SQUARES MARKED OFF IS THE WINNER.

BONUS: YOU CAN ALSO PLAY THIS AS A DRINKING GAME. IT'S SIMPLE. WHEN SOMETHING HAPPENS ON YOUR CARD, YOU HAVE TO TAKE A DRINK. IF YOU MAKE A BINGO—WELL NOW EVERYONE ELSE HAS TO DRINK. JUST MAYBE WAIT UNTIL THE RECEPTION TO START DRINKING. THAT'S WHERE THE OPEN BAR IS ANYWAY.

*DON'T ACTUALLY YELL (OR TALK) DURING A WEDDING.

RECEPTION BIN×GO RECEPTION

THERE ARE COCKTAILS THEMED AFTER THE COUPLE.	SOMEONE SHOUT-SINGS ALONG TO EVERY SONG & NEVER KNOWS THE WORDS.	A DISTANT RELATIVE CLOSE-TALKS WITH THE COUPLE FOR 30 MINUTES.	SOMEONE HAS ON WAY TOO MUCH PERFUME/ COLOGNE.	A POTENTIAL FIST FIGHT ENDS IN AGGRESSIVE HUGGING.
SOMEONE IS EATING AN UNGODLY AMOUNT OF CHEESE.	AN OLDER GRANDPARENT AND/OR DRUNK UNCLE FALLS ASLEEP AT A TABLE.	THE WEDDING DJ PRONOUNCES SOMEONE'S NAME WRONG.	THERE'S A GARTER TOSS AND, YES, IT'S CREEPY.	THERE'S A PHOTO BOOTH, COMPLETE W/ DEMEANING PROPS.
SOMEONE TRIES TO BREAKDANCE & IT DOESN'T END WELL.	2 HOURS IN & SOMEONE STILL HASN'T STOPPED CRYING.	✖	A DRUNK PERSON CONFESSES THEIR LOVE TO SOMEONE.	THERE ARE LAWN GAMES INVOLVED.
THE BRIDAL PARTY SCREAMS LIKE RAPTORS WHEN 'THEIR SONG' COMES ON.	AN ADULT IS SEATED AT THE KIDS TABLE PURELY OUT OF SPITE.	A GUEST TAKES THEIR THIRD TRIP TO THE BUFFET.	A MEMBER OF THE WEDDING PARTY VOMITS.	'SO, HOW LONG DO YOU THINK THIS ONE WILL LAST?'
A GIRL GETS BODY-CHECKED DURING THE BOUQUET TOSS.	THE FATHER DAUGHTER DANCE MUSIC IS A BIT TOO ROMANTIC.	AN ENTIRE TABLE IS ON THEIR PHONES.	SOMEONE HAS WAAAAAY TOO MUCH MAKEUP ON.	SOMEONE GETS CAKE RELENTLESSLY SMASHED IN THEIR FACE.

OBJECTIVE

OH, YOU MEAN BESIDES TRYING TO PASS THE TIME DURING THIS WEDDING THAT YOU MAY OR MAY NOT HAVE EVEN WANTED TO GO TO? ISN'T THAT ENOUGH? WHAT DO YOU WANT FROM US?

WELL, WE HOPE YOU'RE AT LEAST FAMILIAR WITH THE CONCEPT OF BINGO. BECAUSE IF NOT, WELL WE ARE REALLY KIND OF WORRIED ABOUT YOU. WHAT OTHER THINGS IN LIFE HAVE YOU MISSED? SHOES? AUTOMOBILES? TWO-PLY TOILET PAPER? WE DIGRESS.

THIS WEDDING BIN×GO GAME IS PLAYED MUCH LIKE THE TRADITIONAL ONE. YOUR GOAL IS TO SIMPLY BE THE FIRST TO FILL 5 SEQUENTIAL SQUARES IN A ROW, A COLUMN, OR EVEN DIAGONALLY (SEE FIGURE 1 BELOW).

FIGURE 1

SEE THAT X IN THE CENTER SQUARE OF YOUR BOARDS? THAT'S A FREE SQUARE—WHICH MEANS EVERY PLAYER GETS THIS ONE AUTOMATICALLY. IT REALLY HELPS SO...YOU'RE WELCOME

PLAYING THE GAME

AFTER DETERMINING HOW MANY PEOPLE ARE PLAYING, THE OWNER OF THE BOOK SHOULD PERF. OUT A CARD (OR TWO) FOR EVERYONE TO USE AS THEIR PLAY BOARD(S).

ALRIGHT, SO HERE'S HOW OUR GAME IS A BIT DIFFERENT. WE'VE PRE-FILLED EACH CARD WITH THE COMMON (YET RIDICULOUS) THINGS THAT ALWAYS SEEM TO HAPPEN AT THESE EVENTS. SO, INSTEAD OF SOMEONE JUST CALLING OUT NUMBERS, EVERYONE IS PEOPLE WATCHING INSTEAD. WHEN SOMETHING HAPPENS THAT IS ON ONE OF YOUR SQUARES, YOU CALL IT OUT* (AS DISCREETLY AS APPROPRIATE, OF COURSE) AND MARK OFF THE SQUARE. JUST MAKE SURE THE OTHER PLAYERS ARE AWARE.

BY THE WAY, BRIDES & GROOMS TEND TO DO UNIQUELY STUPID THINGS, SO WE PUT THEM IN. ATTENDING A SAME SEX MARRIAGE? AWESOME. FEEL FREE TO MODIFY THE SQUARES AS NEEDED.

WINNING

WHEN A PLAYER MARKS OFF A WINNING CARD, THEY SHOULD YELL* 'BINGO.' IN THE EVENT OF A TIE, THE FIRST TO SAY IT IS THE WINNER. EITHER WAY—EVERYONE ELSE IN THE ROOM WILL PROBABLY BE WONDERING WHAT THE HELL YOU ARE DOING. ADMITTEDLY IT MIGHT BE HARD TO MAKE A TRUE BINGO, SO YOU CAN ALSO DECIDE THAT THE PLAYER WITH THE MOST SQUARES MARKED OFF IS THE WINNER.

BONUS: YOU CAN ALSO PLAY THIS AS A DRINKING GAME. IT'S SIMPLE. WHEN SOMETHING HAPPENS ON YOUR CARD, YOU HAVE TO TAKE A DRINK. IF YOU MAKE A BINGO—WELL NOW EVERYONE ELSE HAS TO DRINK. JUST MAYBE WAIT UNTIL THE RECEPTION TO START DRINKING. THAT'S WHERE THE OPEN BAR IS ANYWAY.

*DON'T ACTUALLY YELL (OR TALK) DURING A WEDDING.

THE WEDDING PARTY IS STANDING IN ORDER OF SHORTEST TO TALLEST.	THE SERMON TAKES LONGER THAN THIRTY MINUTES.	A CLASSICAL VERSION OF A POP SONG IS USED FOR THE AISLE WALK.	SOMEONE IS CRYING SO LOUDLY YOU CAN'T HEAR THE VOWS.	THE VOWS ARE WHISPERED AND HEARD BY ABSOLUTELY NO ONE.
THERE'S A PROP IN THE CEREMONY. CANDLE, SAND, LIVE BIRDS, ETC.	THE KISS HAS TOO MUCH TONGUE.	SOMEONE ACTUALLY OBJECTS.	ONE OF THE PEOPLE GETTING MARRIED JUST DOESN'T SHOW UP.	THE RINGS ARE FORGOTTEN AND/OR LOST.
A CHILD JUST LAYS DOWN IN THE MIDDLE OF THE STAGE.	THE OFFICIANT PRONOUNCES SOMEONE'S NAME WRONG.	✖	THE BRIDE OR GROOM SAID THE WRONG NAME.	SOMEONE MESSES UP THE VOWS.
OH, FUN, A THEME WEDDING.	SOMEONE STILL BRINGS A CHILD TO AN ADULT-ONLY WEDDING.	THE FLOWERS TRIGGERED ALLERGIES & SOMEONE CAN'T STOP SNEEZING.	THE BRIDE TRIPS WHILE WALKING DOWN THE AISLE.	THE BRIDAL PARTY IS DRESSED IN THE LEAST FLATTERING DRESSES.
THE BRIDE IS WEARING 'QUIRKY' SHOES.	THE RINGS ARE DROPPED.	A DOG IS IN THE WEDDING PARTY.	THE DRESS CODE IS CLEARLY JUST MADE-UP, I.E. 'MOUNTAIN SEMI-CASUAL'	EVERYONE AT THE ALTAR HAS THEIR OWN MICROPHONE.

OBJECTIVE

OH, YOU MEAN BESIDES TRYING TO PASS THE TIME DURING THIS WEDDING THAT YOU MAY OR MAY NOT HAVE EVEN WANTED TO GO TO? ISN'T THAT ENOUGH? WHAT DO YOU WANT FROM US?

WELL, WE HOPE YOU'RE AT LEAST FAMILIAR WITH THE CONCEPT OF BINGO. BECAUSE IF NOT, WELL WE ARE REALLY KIND OF WORRIED ABOUT YOU. WHAT OTHER THINGS IN LIFE HAVE YOU MISSED? SHOES? AUTOMOBILES? TWO-PLY TOILET PAPER? WE DIGRESS.

THIS WEDDING BIN×GO GAME IS PLAYED MUCH LIKE THE TRADITIONAL ONE. YOUR GOAL IS TO SIMPLY BE THE FIRST TO FILL 5 SEQUENTIAL SQUARES IN A ROW, A COLUMN, OR EVEN DIAGONALLY (SEE FIGURE 1 BELOW).

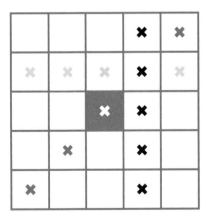

FIGURE 1

SEE THAT X IN THE CENTER SQUARE OF YOUR BOARDS? THAT'S A FREE SQUARE—WHICH MEANS EVERY PLAYER GETS THIS ONE AUTOMATICALLY. IT REALLY HELPS SO...YOU'RE WELCOME

PLAYING THE GAME

AFTER DETERMINING HOW MANY PEOPLE ARE PLAYING, THE OWNER OF THE BOOK SHOULD PERF. OUT A CARD (OR TWO) FOR EVERYONE TO USE AS THEIR PLAY BOARD(S).

ALRIGHT, SO HERE'S HOW OUR GAME IS A BIT DIFFERENT. WE'VE PRE-FILLED EACH CARD WITH THE COMMON (YET RIDICULOUS) THINGS THAT ALWAYS SEEM TO HAPPEN AT THESE EVENTS. SO, INSTEAD OF SOMEONE JUST CALLING OUT NUMBERS, EVERYONE IS PEOPLE WATCHING INSTEAD. WHEN SOMETHING HAPPENS THAT IS ON ONE OF YOUR SQUARES, YOU CALL IT OUT* (AS DISCREETLY AS APPROPRIATE, OF COURSE) AND MARK OFF THE SQUARE. JUST MAKE THE OTHER PLAYERS ARE AWARE.

BY THE WAY, BRIDES & GROOMS TEND TO DO UNIQUELY STUPID THINGS, SO WE PUT THEM IN. ATTENDING A SAME SEX MARRIAGE? AWESOME. FEEL FREE TO MODIFY THE SQUARES AS NEEDED.

WINNING

WHEN A PLAYER MARKS OFF A WINNING CARD, THEY SHOULD YELL* 'BINGO.' IN THE EVENT OF A TIE, THE FIRST TO SAY IT IS THE WINNER. EITHER WAY—EVERYONE ELSE IN THE ROOM WILL PROBABLY BE WONDERING WHAT THE HELL YOU ARE DOING. ADMITTEDLY IT MIGHT BE HARD TO MAKE A TRUE BINGO, SO YOU CAN ALSO DECIDE THAT THE PLAYER WITH THE MOST SQUARES MARKED OFF IS THE WINNER.

BONUS: YOU CAN ALSO PLAY THIS AS A DRINKING GAME. IT'S SIMPLE. WHEN SOMETHING HAPPENS ON YOUR CARD, YOU HAVE TO TAKE A DRINK. IF YOU MAKE A BINGO—WELL NOW EVERYONE ELSE HAS TO DRINK. JUST MAYBE WAIT UNTIL THE RECEPTION TO START DRINKING. THAT'S WHERE THE OPEN BAR IS ANYWAY.

*DON'T ACTUALLY YELL (OR TALK) DURING A WEDDING.

SOMETHING IMPORTANT BLOWS AWAY DURING AN OUTDOOR CEREMONY.	THE PROGRAM HAS MULTIPLE PAGES.	THE VOWS FEATURE A QUOTE FROM 'THE NOTEBOOK.'	THE GROOMSMEN ARE ALL WEARING SUSPENDERS.	THE WEDDING STARTS AT LEAST THIRTY MINUTES LATE.
SOMEONE IS USING THE PROGRAM AS A FAN.	'LOVE IS PATIENT. LOVE IS KIND.'	RING BEARER OR FLOWER GIRL CAN'T MAKE IT DOWN THE AISLE.	A MEMBER OF THE WEDDING PARTY IS OBVIOUSLY HUNGOVER.	THE COUPLE AWKWARDLY DANCES DOWN THE AISLE AFTER BEING ANNOUNCED.
A CHILD FACE-PLANTS BEFORE REACHING THE END OF THE AISLE.	THE WEDDING PROCESSION WALKS AT THE SPEED OF LIGHT.	✖	A WILDLY UNDERDRESSED GUEST SHOWS UP.	YOU HAVE TO STAND UP & SIT DOWN ROUGHLY 100 TIMES.
'FOR RICHER OR FOR RICHER.'	A MEMBER OF THE WEDDING PARTY IS CURRENTLY INEBRIATED.	SOMEONE SINGS A HEARTFELT SONG. IT'S NOT IN KEY.	THE WHOLE THING LASTS FOR OVER TWO HOURS.	THE VOWS TAKE AT LEAST 5 MINUTES. EACH.
AN AUDIENCE MEMBER HAS CLEARLY FALLEN ASLEEP.	SOMEONE IS ALREADY DRINKING FROM A FLASK.	TOO MUCH ENERGY IS SPENT KEEPING DIVORCED PARENTS APART.	THE MOTHER OF THE GROOM SPENDS MOST OF HER TIME GLARING AT THE BRIDE.	SOMEONE CRIES BEFORE, DURING & AFTER THE CEREMONY.

OBJECTIVE

OH, YOU MEAN BESIDES TRYING TO PASS THE TIME DURING THIS WEDDING THAT YOU MAY OR MAY NOT HAVE EVEN WANTED TO GO TO? ISN'T THAT ENOUGH? WHAT DO YOU WANT FROM US?

WELL, WE HOPE YOU'RE AT LEAST FAMILIAR WITH THE CONCEPT OF BINGO. BECAUSE IF NOT, WELL WE ARE REALLY KIND OF WORRIED ABOUT YOU. WHAT OTHER THINGS IN LIFE HAVE YOU MISSED? SHOES? AUTOMOBILES? TWO-PLY TOILET PAPER? WE DIGRESS.

THIS WEDDING BIN×GO GAME IS PLAYED MUCH LIKE THE TRADITIONAL ONE. YOUR GOAL IS TO SIMPLY BE THE FIRST TO FILL 5 SEQUENTIAL SQUARES IN A ROW, A COLUMN, OR EVEN DIAGONALLY (SEE FIGURE 1 BELOW).

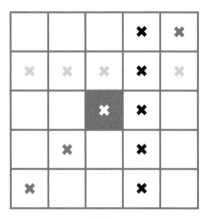

FIGURE 1

SEE THAT X IN THE CENTER SQUARE OF YOUR BOARDS? THAT'S A FREE SQUARE—WHICH MEANS EVERY PLAYER GETS THIS ONE AUTOMATICALLY. IT REALLY HELPS SO...YOU'RE WELCOME

PLAYING THE GAME

AFTER DETERMINING HOW MANY PEOPLE ARE PLAYING, THE OWNER OF THE BOOK SHOULD PERF. OUT A CARD (OR TWO) FOR EVERYONE TO USE AS THEIR PLAY BOARD(S).

ALRIGHT, SO HERE'S HOW OUR GAME IS A BIT DIFFERENT. WE'VE PRE-FILLED EACH CARD WITH THE COMMON (YET RIDICULOUS) THINGS THAT ALWAYS SEEM TO HAPPEN AT THESE EVENTS. SO, INSTEAD OF SOMEONE JUST CALLING OUT NUMBERS, EVERYONE IS PEOPLE WATCHING INSTEAD. WHEN SOMETHING HAPPENS THAT IS ON ONE OF YOUR SQUARES, YOU CALL IT OUT* (AS DISCREETLY AS APPROPRIATE, OF COURSE) AND MARK OFF THE SQUARE. JUST MAKE THE OTHER PLAYERS ARE AWARE.

BY THE WAY, BRIDES & GROOMS TEND TO DO UNIQUELY STUPID THINGS, SO WE PUT THEM IN. ATTENDING A SAME SEX MARRIAGE? AWESOME. FEEL FREE TO MODIFY THE SQUARES AS NEEDED.

WINNING

WHEN A PLAYER MARKS OFF A WINNING CARD, THEY SHOULD YELL*'BINGO.' IN THE EVENT OF A TIE, THE FIRST TO SAY IT IS THE WINNER. EITHER WAY—EVERYONE ELSE IN THE ROOM WILL PROBABLY BE WONDERING WHAT THE HELL YOU ARE DOING. ADMITTEDLY IT MIGHT BE HARD TO MAKE A TRUE BINGO, SO YOU CAN ALSO DECIDE THAT THE PLAYER WITH THE MOST SQUARES MARKED OFF IS THE WINNER.

BONUS: YOU CAN ALSO PLAY THIS AS A DRINKING GAME. IT'S SIMPLE. WHEN SOMETHING HAPPENS ON YOUR CARD, YOU HAVE TO TAKE A DRINK. IF YOU MAKE A BINGO—WELL NOW EVERYONE ELSE HAS TO DRINK. JUST MAYBE WAIT UNTIL THE RECEPTION TO START DRINKING. THAT'S WHERE THE OPEN BAR IS ANYWAY.

*DON'T ACTUALLY YELL (OR TALK) DURING A WEDDING.

WEDDING **BIN×GO** WEDDING

THE OFFICIANT PRONOUNCES SOMEONE'S NAME WRONG.	THE KISS HAS TOO MUCH TONGUE.	THE WEDDING STARTS AT LEAST THIRTY MINUTES LATE.	THE SERMON TAKES LONGER THAN THIRTY MINUTES.	SOMEONE IS USING THE PROGRAM AS A FAN.
THE VOWS ARE WHISPERED AND HEARD BY ABSOLUTELY NO ONE.	THE COUPLE AWKWARDLY DANCES DOWN THE AISLE AFTER BEING ANNOUNCED.	THE BRIDE TRIPS WHILE WALKING DOWN THE AISLE.	SOMEONE SINGS A HEARTFELT SONG. IT'S NOT IN KEY.	THE VOWS TAKE AT LEAST 5 MINUTES. EACH.
SOMEONE MESSES UP THE VOWS.	A MEMBER OF THE WEDDING PARTY IS CURRENTLY INEBRIATED.	✖	A DOG IS IN THE WEDDING PARTY.	THE BRIDAL PARTY IS DRESSED IN THE LEAST FLATTERING DRESSES.
THE RINGS ARE DROPPED.	THE WEDDING PROCESSION WALKS AT THE SPEED OF LIGHT.	THE RINGS ARE FORGOTTEN AND/OR LOST.	THE DRESS CODE IS CLEARLY JUST MADE-UP. I.E. 'MOUNTAIN SEMI-CASUAL'	SOMEONE STILL BRINGS A CHILD TO AN ADULT-ONLY WEDDING.
SOMEONE CRIES BEFORE, DURING & AFTER THE CEREMONY.	SOMEONE IS ALREADY DRINKING FROM A FLASK.	THE WEDDING PARTY IS STANDING IN ORDER OF SHORTEST TO TALLEST.	SOMEONE IS CRYING SO LOUDLY YOU CAN'T HEAR THE VOWS.	EVERYONE AT THE ALTAR HAS THEIR OWN MICROPHONE.

OBJECTIVE

OH, YOU MEAN BESIDES TRYING TO PASS THE TIME DURING THIS WEDDING THAT YOU MAY OR MAY NOT HAVE EVEN WANTED TO GO TO? ISN'T THAT ENOUGH? WHAT DO YOU WANT FROM US?

WELL, WE HOPE YOU'RE AT LEAST FAMILIAR WITH THE CONCEPT OF BINGO, BECAUSE IF NOT, WELL WE ARE REALLY KIND OF WORRIED ABOUT YOU. WHAT OTHER THINGS IN LIFE HAVE YOU MISSED? SHOES? AUTOMOBILES? TWO-PLY TOILET PAPER? WE DIGRESS.

THIS WEDDING BIN×GO GAME IS PLAYED MUCH LIKE THE TRADITIONAL ONE. YOUR GOAL IS TO SIMPLY BE THE FIRST TO FILL 5 SEQUENTIAL SQUARES IN A ROW, A COLUMN, OR EVEN DIAGONALLY (SEE FIGURE 1 BELOW).

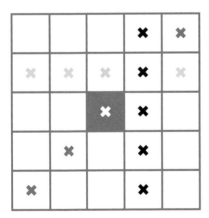

FIGURE 1

SEE THAT X IN THE CENTER SQUARE OF YOUR BOARDS? THAT'S A FREE SQUARE—WHICH MEANS EVERY PLAYER GETS THIS ONE AUTOMATICALLY. IT REALLY HELPS SO...YOU'RE WELCOME

PLAYING THE GAME

AFTER DETERMINING HOW MANY PEOPLE ARE PLAYING, THE OWNER OF THE BOOK SHOULD PERF. OUT A CARD (OR TWO) FOR EVERYONE TO USE AS THEIR PLAY BOARD(S).

ALRIGHT, SO HERE'S HOW OUR GAME IS A BIT DIFFERENT. WE'VE PRE-FILLED EACH CARD WITH THE COMMON (YET RIDICULOUS) THINGS THAT ALWAYS SEEM TO HAPPEN AT THESE EVENTS. SO, INSTEAD OF SOMEONE JUST CALLING OUT NUMBERS, EVERYONE IS PEOPLE WATCHING INSTEAD. WHEN SOMETHING HAPPENS THAT IS ON ONE OF YOUR SQUARES, YOU CALL IT OUT* (AS DISCREETLY AS APPROPRIATE, OF COURSE) AND MARK OFF THE SQUARE. JUST MAKE THE OTHER PLAYERS ARE AWARE.

BY THE WAY, BRIDES & GROOMS TEND TO DO UNIQUELY STUPID THINGS, SO WE PUT THEM IN. ATTENDING A SAME SEX MARRIAGE? AWESOME. FEEL FREE TO MODIFY THE SQUARES AS NEEDED.

WINNING

WHEN A PLAYER MARKS OFF A WINNING CARD, THEY SHOULD YELL* 'BINGO.' IN THE EVENT OF A TIE, THE FIRST TO SAY IT IS THE WINNER. EITHER WAY—EVERYONE ELSE IN THE ROOM WILL PROBABLY BE WONDERING WHAT THE HELL YOU ARE DOING. ADMITTEDLY IT MIGHT BE HARD TO MAKE A TRUE BINGO, SO YOU CAN ALSO DECIDE THAT THE PLAYER WITH THE MOST SQUARES MARKED OFF IS THE WINNER.

BONUS: YOU CAN ALSO PLAY THIS AS A DRINKING GAME. IT'S SIMPLE. WHEN SOMETHING HAPPENS ON YOUR CARD, YOU HAVE TO TAKE A DRINK. IF YOU MAKE A BINGO—WELL NOW EVERYONE ELSE HAS TO DRINK. JUST MAYBE WAIT UNTIL THE RECEPTION TO START DRINKING. THAT'S WHERE THE OPEN BAR IS ANYWAY.

*DON'T ACTUALLY YELL (OR TALK) DURING A WEDDING.

THE BRIDAL PARTY IS DRESSED IN THE LEAST FLATTERING DRESSES.	'FOR RICHER OR FOR RICHER.'	THE MOTHER OF THE GROOM SPENDS MOST OF HER TIME GLARING AT THE BRIDE.	'LOVE IS PATIENT, LOVE IS KIND.'	THE RINGS ARE DROPPED.
A CHILD JUST LAYS DOWN IN THE MIDDLE OF THE STAGE.	THE OFFICIANT PRONOUNCES SOMEONE'S NAME WRONG.	THE PROGRAM HAS MULTIPLE PAGES.	THE VOWS FEATURE A QUOTE FROM 'THE NOTEBOOK.'	EVERYONE AT THE ALTAR HAS THEIR OWN MICROPHONE.
SOMEONE MESSES UP THE VOWS.	SOMEONE IS ALREADY DRINKING FROM A FLASK.	✖	YOU HAVE TO STAND UP & SIT DOWN ROUGHLY 100 TIMES.	SOMEONE SINGS A HEARTFELT SONG. IT'S NOT IN KEY.
SOMEONE STILL BRINGS A CHILD TO AN ADULT-ONLY WEDDING.	SOMEONE IS USING THE PROGRAM AS A FAN.	THE WHOLE THING LASTS FOR OVER TWO HOURS.	A CLASSICAL VERSION OF A POP SONG IS USED FOR THE AISLE WALK.	THE DRESS CODE IS CLEARLY JUST MADE-UP, I.E. 'MOUNTAIN SEMI-CASUAL.'
THE VOWS ARE WHISPERED AND HEARD BY ABSOLUTELY NO ONE.	TOO MUCH ENERGY IS SPENT KEEPING DIVORCED PARENTS APART.	THERE'S A PROP IN THE CEREMONY. CANDLE, SAND, LIVE BIRDS, ETC.	SOMETHING IMPORTANT BLOWS AWAY DURING AN OUTDOOR CEREMONY.	THE VOWS TAKE AT LEAST 5 MINUTES. EACH.

OBJECTIVE

OH, YOU MEAN BESIDES TRYING TO PASS THE TIME DURING THIS WEDDING THAT YOU MAY OR MAY NOT HAVE EVEN WANTED TO GO TO? ISN'T THAT ENOUGH? WHAT DO YOU WANT FROM US?

WELL, WE HOPE YOU'RE AT LEAST FAMILIAR WITH THE CONCEPT OF BINGO. BECAUSE IF NOT, WELL WE ARE REALLY KIND OF WORRIED ABOUT YOU. WHAT OTHER THINGS IN LIFE HAVE YOU MISSED? SHOES? AUTOMOBILES? TWO-PLY TOILET PAPER? WE DIGRESS.

THIS WEDDING BIN×GO GAME IS PLAYED MUCH LIKE THE TRADITIONAL ONE. YOUR GOAL IS TO SIMPLY BE THE FIRST TO FILL 5 SEQUENTIAL SQUARES IN A ROW, A COLUMN, OR EVEN DIAGONALLY (SEE FIGURE 1 BELOW).

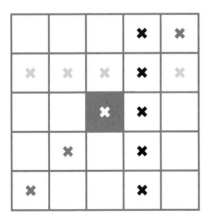

FIGURE 1

SEE THAT X IN THE CENTER SQUARE OF YOUR BOARDS? THAT'S A FREE SQUARE—WHICH MEANS EVERY PLAYER GETS THIS ONE AUTOMATICALLY. IT REALLY HELPS SO...YOU'RE WELCOME

PLAYING THE GAME

AFTER DETERMINING HOW MANY PEOPLE ARE PLAYING, THE OWNER OF THE BOOK SHOULD PERF. OUT A CARD (OR TWO) FOR EVERYONE TO USE AS THEIR PLAY BOARD(S).

ALRIGHT, SO HERE'S HOW OUR GAME IS A BIT DIFFERENT. WE'VE PRE-FILLED EACH CARD WITH THE COMMON (YET RIDICULOUS) THINGS THAT ALWAYS SEEM TO HAPPEN AT THESE EVENTS. SO, INSTEAD OF SOMEONE JUST CALLING OUT NUMBERS, EVERYONE IS PEOPLE WATCHING INSTEAD. WHEN SOMETHING HAPPENS THAT IS ON ONE OF YOUR SQUARES, YOU CALL IT OUT* (AS DISCREETLY AS APPROPRIATE, OF COURSE) AND MARK OFF THE SQUARE. JUST MAKE THE OTHER PLAYERS ARE AWARE.

BY THE WAY, BRIDES & GROOMS TEND TO DO UNIQUELY STUPID THINGS, SO WE PUT THEM IN. ATTENDING A SAME SEX MARRIAGE? AWESOME. FEEL FREE TO MODIFY THE SQUARES AS NEEDED.

WINNING

WHEN A PLAYER MARKS OFF A WINNING CARD, THEY SHOULD YELL* 'BINGO.' IN THE EVENT OF A TIE, THE FIRST TO SAY IT IS THE WINNER. EITHER WAY—EVERYONE ELSE IN THE ROOM WILL PROBABLY BE WONDERING WHAT THE HELL YOU ARE DOING. ADMITTEDLY IT MIGHT BE HARD TO MAKE A TRUE BINGO, SO YOU CAN ALSO DECIDE THAT THE PLAYER WITH THE MOST SQUARES MARKED OFF IS THE WINNER.

BONUS: YOU CAN ALSO PLAY THIS AS A DRINKING GAME. IT'S SIMPLE. WHEN SOMETHING HAPPENS ON YOUR CARD, YOU HAVE TO TAKE A DRINK. IF YOU MAKE A BINGO—WELL NOW EVERYONE ELSE HAS TO DRINK. JUST MAYBE WAIT UNTIL THE RECEPTION TO START DRINKING. THAT'S WHERE THE OPEN BAR IS ANYWAY.

*DON'T ACTUALLY YELL (OR TALK) DURING A WEDDING.

WEDDING BIN×GO WEDDING

A CLASSICAL VERSION OF A POP SONG IS USED FOR THE AISLE WALK.	THE BRIDAL PARTY IS DRESSED IN THE LEAST FLATTERING DRESSES.	SOMEONE CRIES BEFORE, DURING & AFTER THE CEREMONY.	A DOG IS IN THE WEDDING PARTY.	THE COUPLE AWKWARDLY DANCES DOWN THE AISLE AFTER BEING ANNOUNCED.
A MEMBER OF THE WEDDING PARTY IS OBVIOUSLY HUNGOVER.	THE BRIDE IS WEARING 'QUIRKY' SHOES.	A CHILD FACE-PLANTS BEFORE REACHING THE END OF THE AISLE.	SOMEONE SINGS A HEARTFELT SONG. IT'S NOT IN KEY.	SOMEONE IS USING THE PROGRAM AS A FAN.
THE GROOMSMEN ARE ALL WEARING SUSPENDERS.	SOMEONE ACTUALLY OBJECTS.	✖	'FOR RICHER OR FOR RICHER.'	THE WHOLE THING LASTS FOR OVER TWO HOURS.
'LOVE IS PATIENT, LOVE IS KIND.'	AN AUDIENCE MEMBER HAS CLEARLY FALLEN ASLEEP.	OH, FUN, A THEME WEDDING.	THE VOWS ARE WHISPERED AND HEARD BY ABSOLUTELY NO ONE.	THE WEDDING PROCESSION WALKS AT THE SPEED OF LIGHT.
THE WEDDING PARTY IS STANDING IN ORDER OF SHORTEST TO TALLEST.	A WILDLY UNDERDRESSED GUEST SHOWS UP.	A CHILD JUST LAYS DOWN IN THE MIDDLE OF THE STAGE.	THE KISS HAS TOO MUCH TONGUE.	SOMEONE STILL BRINGS A CHILD TO AN ADULT-ONLY WEDDING.

OBJECTIVE

OH, YOU MEAN BESIDES TRYING TO PASS THE TIME DURING THIS WEDDING THAT YOU MAY OR MAY NOT HAVE EVEN WANTED TO GO TO? ISN'T THAT ENOUGH? WHAT DO YOU WANT FROM US?

WELL, WE HOPE YOU'RE AT LEAST FAMILIAR WITH THE CONCEPT OF BINGO. BECAUSE IF NOT, WELL WE ARE REALLY KIND OF WORRIED ABOUT YOU. WHAT OTHER THINGS IN LIFE HAVE YOU MISSED? SHOES? AUTOMOBILES? TWO-PLY TOILET PAPER? WE DIGRESS.

THIS WEDDING BIN·GO GAME IS PLAYED MUCH LIKE THE TRADITIONAL ONE. YOUR GOAL IS TO SIMPLY BE THE FIRST TO FILL 5 SEQUENTIAL SQUARES IN A ROW, A COLUMN, OR EVEN DIAGONALLY (SEE FIGURE 1 BELOW).

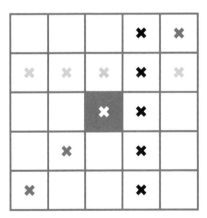

FIGURE 1

SEE THAT X IN THE CENTER SQUARE OF YOUR BOARDS? THAT'S A FREE SQUARE—WHICH MEANS EVERY PLAYER GETS THIS ONE AUTOMATICALLY. IT REALLY HELPS SO...YOU'RE WELCOME

PLAYING THE GAME

AFTER DETERMINING HOW MANY PEOPLE ARE PLAYING, THE OWNER OF THE BOOK SHOULD PERF. OUT A CARD (OR TWO) FOR EVERYONE TO USE AS THEIR PLAY BOARD(S).

ALRIGHT, SO HERE'S HOW OUR GAME IS A BIT DIFFERENT. WE'VE PRE-FILLED EACH CARD WITH THE COMMON (YET RIDICULOUS) THINGS THAT ALWAYS SEEM TO HAPPEN AT THESE EVENTS. SO, INSTEAD OF SOMEONE JUST CALLING OUT NUMBERS, EVERYONE IS PEOPLE WATCHING INSTEAD. WHEN SOMETHING HAPPENS THAT IS ON ONE OF YOUR SQUARES, YOU CALL IT OUT* (AS DISCRETELY AS APPROPRIATE, OF COURSE) AND MARK OFF THE SQUARE. JUST MAKE THE OTHER PLAYERS ARE AWARE.

BY THE WAY, BRIDES & GROOMS TEND TO DO UNIQUELY STUPID THINGS, SO WE PUT THEM IN. ATTENDING A SAME SEX MARRIAGE? AWESOME. FEEL FREE TO MODIFY THE SQUARES AS NEEDED.

WINNING

WHEN A PLAYER MARKS OFF A WINNING CARD, THEY SHOULD YELL* 'BINGO.' IN THE EVENT OF A TIE, THE FIRST TO SAY IT IS THE WINNER. EITHER WAY—EVERYONE ELSE IN THE ROOM WILL PROBABLY BE WONDERING WHAT THE HELL YOU ARE DOING. ADMITTEDLY IT MIGHT BE HARD TO MAKE A TRUE BINGO, SO YOU CAN ALSO DECIDE THAT THE PLAYER WITH THE MOST SQUARES MARKED OFF IS THE WINNER.

BONUS: YOU CAN ALSO PLAY THIS AS A DRINKING GAME. IT'S SIMPLE. WHEN SOMETHING HAPPENS ON YOUR CARD, YOU HAVE TO TAKE A DRINK. IF YOU MAKE A BINGO—WELL NOW EVERYONE ELSE HAS TO DRINK. JUST MAYBE WAIT UNTIL THE RECEPTION TO START DRINKING. THAT'S WHERE THE OPEN BAR IS ANYWAY.

*DON'T ACTUALLY YELL (OR TALK) DURING A WEDDING.

THE WEDDING PARTY IS STANDING IN ORDER OF SHORTEST TO TALLEST.	THE GROOMSMEN ARE ALL WEARING SUSPENDERS.	A MEMBER OF THE WEDDING PARTY IS OBVIOUSLY HUNGOVER.	THE WEDDING PROCESSION WALKS AT THE SPEED OF LIGHT.	SOMEONE CRIES BEFORE, DURING & AFTER THE CEREMONY.
SOMETHING IMPORTANT BLOWS AWAY DURING AN OUTDOOR CEREMONY.	THE DRESS CODE IS CLEARLY JUST MADE-UP. I.E. 'MOUNTAIN SEMI-CASUAL'	THE SERMON TAKES LONGER THAN THIRTY MINUTES.	A CHILD JUST LAYS DOWN IN THE MIDDLE OF THE STAGE.	SOMEONE SINGS A HEARTFELT SONG. IT'S NOT IN KEY.
THE RINGS ARE FORGOTTEN AND/OR LOST.	SOMEONE IS CRYING SO LOUDLY YOU CAN'T HEAR THE VOWS.	✖	'LOVE IS PATIENT, LOVE IS KIND.'	THE VOWS FEATURE A QUOTE FROM 'THE NOTEBOOK.'
THE BRIDE TRIPS WHILE WALKING DOWN THE AISLE.	THE VOWS TAKE AT LEAST 5 MINUTES, EACH.	THE WHOLE THING LASTS FOR OVER TWO HOURS.	THERE'S A PROP IN THE CEREMONY. CANDLE, SAND, LIVE BIRDS, ETC.	A CLASSICAL VERSION OF A POP SONG IS USED FOR THE AISLE WALK.
THE OFFICIANT PRONOUNCES SOMEONE'S NAME WRONG.	THE BRIDAL PARTY IS DRESSED IN THE LEAST FLATTERING DRESSES.	YOU HAVE TO STAND UP & SIT DOWN ROUGHLY 100 TIMES.	SOMEONE STILL BRINGS A CHILD TO AN ADULT-ONLY WEDDING.	A WILDLY UNDERDRESSED GUEST SHOWS UP.

OBJECTIVE

OH, YOU MEAN BESIDES TRYING TO PASS THE TIME DURING THIS WEDDING THAT YOU MAY OR MAY NOT HAVE EVEN WANTED TO GO TO? ISN'T THAT ENOUGH? WHAT DO YOU WANT FROM US?

WELL, WE HOPE YOU'RE AT LEAST FAMILIAR WITH THE CONCEPT OF BINGO. BECAUSE IF NOT, WELL WE ARE REALLY KIND OF WORRIED ABOUT YOU. WHAT OTHER THINGS IN LIFE HAVE YOU MISSED? SHOES? AUTOMOBILES? TWO-PLY TOILET PAPER? WE DIGRESS.

THIS WEDDING BIN·GO GAME IS PLAYED MUCH LIKE THE TRADITIONAL ONE. YOUR GOAL IS TO SIMPLY BE THE FIRST TO FILL 5 SEQUENTIAL SQUARES IN A ROW, A COLUMN, OR EVEN DIAGONALLY (SEE FIGURE 1 BELOW).

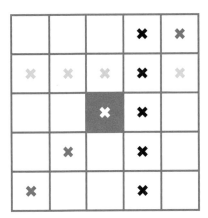

FIGURE 1

SEE THAT X IN THE CENTER SQUARE OF YOUR BOARDS? THAT'S A FREE SQUARE—WHICH MEANS EVERY PLAYER GETS THIS ONE AUTOMATICALLY. IT REALLY HELPS SO...YOU'RE WELCOME

PLAYING THE GAME

AFTER DETERMINING HOW MANY PEOPLE ARE PLAYING, THE OWNER OF THE BOOK SHOULD PERF. OUT A CARD (OR TWO) FOR EVERYONE TO USE AS THEIR PLAY BOARD(S).

ALRIGHT, SO HERE'S HOW OUR GAME IS A BIT DIFFERENT. WE'VE PRE-FILLED EACH CARD WITH THE COMMON (YET RIDICULOUS) THINGS THAT ALWAYS SEEM TO HAPPEN AT THESE EVENTS. SO, INSTEAD OF SOMEONE JUST CALLING OUT NUMBERS, EVERYONE IS PEOPLE WATCHING INSTEAD. WHEN SOMETHING HAPPENS THAT IS ON ONE OF YOUR SQUARES, YOU CALL IT OUT* (AS DISCREETLY AS APPROPRIATE, OF COURSE) AND MARK OFF THE SQUARE. JUST MAKE THE OTHER PLAYERS ARE AWARE.

BY THE WAY, BRIDES & GROOMS TEND TO DO UNIQUELY STUPID THINGS, SO WE PUT THEM IN. ATTENDING A SAME SEX MARRIAGE? AWESOME. FEEL FREE TO MODIFY THE SQUARES AS NEEDED.

WINNING

WHEN A PLAYER MARKS OFF A WINNING CARD, THEY SHOULD YELL* 'BINGO.' IN THE EVENT OF A TIE, THE FIRST TO SAY IT IS THE WINNER. EITHER WAY—EVERYONE ELSE IN THE ROOM WILL PROBABLY BE WONDERING WHAT THE HELL YOU ARE DOING. ADMITTEDLY IT MIGHT BE HARD TO MAKE A TRUE BINGO, SO YOU CAN ALSO DECIDE THAT THE PLAYER WITH THE MOST SQUARES MARKED OFF IS THE WINNER.

BONUS: YOU CAN ALSO PLAY THIS AS A DRINKING GAME. IT'S SIMPLE. WHEN SOMETHING HAPPENS ON YOUR CARD, YOU HAVE TO TAKE A DRINK. IF YOU MAKE A BINGO—WELL NOW EVERYONE ELSE HAS TO DRINK. JUST MAYBE WAIT UNTIL THE RECEPTION TO START DRINKING. THAT'S WHERE THE OPEN BAR IS ANYWAY.

*DON'T ACTUALLY YELL (OR TALK) DURING A WEDDING.

THE WEDDING PARTY IS STANDING IN ORDER OF SHORTEST TO TALLEST.	THE RINGS ARE FORGOTTEN AND/OR LOST.	THE SERMON TAKES LONGER THAN THIRTY MINUTES.	THE FLOWERS TRIGGERED ALLERGIES & SOMEONE CAN'T STOP SNEEZING.	YOU HAVE TO STAND UP & SIT DOWN ROUGHLY 100 TIMES.
SOMEONE SINGS A HEARTFELT SONG. IT'S NOT IN KEY.	A MEMBER OF THE WEDDING PARTY IS OBVIOUSLY HUNGOVER.	SOMEONE STILL BRINGS A CHILD TO AN ADULT-ONLY WEDDING.	A CHILD FACE-PLANTS BEFORE REACHING THE END OF THE AISLE.	SOMEONE IS ALREADY DRINKING FROM A FLASK.
RING BEARER OR FLOWER GIRL CAN'T MAKE IT DOWN THE AISLE.	THE BRIDAL PARTY IS DRESSED IN THE LEAST FLATTERING DRESSES.	✖	THE WEDDING PROCESSION WALKS AT THE SPEED OF LIGHT.	SOMEONE IS USING THE PROGRAM AS A FAN.
SOMEONE IS CRYING SO LOUDLY YOU CAN'T HEAR THE VOWS.	THE RINGS ARE DROPPED.	OH, FUN. A THEME WEDDING.	'FOR RICHER OR FOR RICHER.'	A WILDLY UNDERDRESSED GUEST SHOWS UP.
THE KISS HAS TOO MUCH TONGUE.	SOMEONE ACTUALLY OBJECTS.	SOMETHING IMPORTANT BLOWS AWAY DURING AN OUTDOOR CEREMONY.	THERE'S A PROP IN THE CEREMONY. CANDLE. SAND. LIVE BIRDS. ETC.	SOMEONE MESSES UP THE VOWS.

OBJECTIVE

OH, YOU MEAN BESIDES TRYING TO PASS THE TIME DURING THIS WEDDING THAT YOU MAY OR MAY NOT HAVE EVEN WANTED TO GO TO? ISN'T THAT ENOUGH? WHAT DO YOU WANT FROM US?

WELL, WE HOPE YOU'RE AT LEAST FAMILIAR WITH THE CONCEPT OF BINGO. BECAUSE IF NOT, WELL WE ARE REALLY KIND OF WORRIED ABOUT YOU. WHAT OTHER THINGS IN LIFE HAVE YOU MISSED? SHOES? AUTOMOBILES? TWO-PLY TOILET PAPER? WE DIGRESS.

THIS WEDDING BIN×GO GAME IS PLAYED MUCH LIKE THE TRADITIONAL ONE. YOUR GOAL IS TO SIMPLY BE THE FIRST TO FILL 5 SEQUENTIAL SQUARES IN A ROW, A COLUMN, OR EVEN DIAGONALLY (SEE FIGURE 1 BELOW).

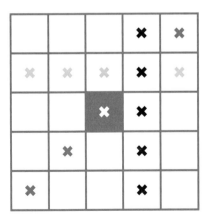

FIGURE 1

SEE THAT X IN THE CENTER SQUARE OF YOUR BOARDS? THAT'S A FREE SQUARE—WHICH MEANS EVERY PLAYER GETS THIS ONE AUTOMATICALLY. IT REALLY HELPS SO...YOU'RE WELCOME

PLAYING THE GAME

AFTER DETERMINING HOW MANY PEOPLE ARE PLAYING, THE OWNER OF THE BOOK SHOULD PERF. OUT A CARD (OR TWO) FOR EVERYONE TO USE AS THEIR PLAY BOARD(S).

ALRIGHT, SO HERE'S HOW OUR GAME IS A BIT DIFFERENT. WE'VE PRE-FILLED EACH CARD WITH THE COMMON (YET RIDICULOUS) THINGS THAT ALWAYS SEEM TO HAPPEN AT THESE EVENTS. SO, INSTEAD OF SOMEONE JUST CALLING OUT NUMBERS, EVERYONE IS PEOPLE WATCHING INSTEAD. WHEN SOMETHING HAPPENS THAT IS ON ONE OF YOUR SQUARES, YOU CALL IT OUT* (AS DISCREETLY AS APPROPRIATE, OF COURSE) AND MARK OFF THE SQUARE. JUST MAKE THE OTHER PLAYERS ARE AWARE.

BY THE WAY, BRIDES & GROOMS TEND TO DO UNIQUELY STUPID THINGS, SO WE PUT THEM IN. ATTENDING A SAME SEX MARRIAGE? AWESOME. FEEL FREE TO MODIFY THE SQUARES AS NEEDED.

WINNING

WHEN A PLAYER MARKS OFF A WINNING CARD, THEY SHOULD YELL* 'BINGO.' IN THE EVENT OF A TIE, THE FIRST TO SAY IT IS THE WINNER. EITHER WAY—EVERYONE ELSE IN THE ROOM WILL PROBABLY BE WONDERING WHAT THE HELL YOU ARE DOING. ADMITTEDLY IT MIGHT BE HARD TO MAKE A TRUE BINGO, SO YOU CAN ALSO DECIDE THAT THE PLAYER WITH THE MOST SQUARES MARKED OFF IS THE WINNER.

BONUS: YOU CAN ALSO PLAY THIS AS A DRINKING GAME. IT'S SIMPLE. WHEN SOMETHING HAPPENS ON YOUR CARD, YOU HAVE TO TAKE A DRINK. IF YOU MAKE A BINGO—WELL NOW EVERYONE ELSE HAS TO DRINK. JUST MAYBE WAIT UNTIL THE RECEPTION TO START DRINKING. THAT'S WHERE THE OPEN BAR IS ANYWAY.

*DON'T ACTUALLY YELL (OR TALK) DURING A WEDDING.

RING BEARER OR FLOWER GIRL CAN'T MAKE IT DOWN THE AISLE.	AN AUDIENCE MEMBER HAS CLEARLY FALLEN ASLEEP.	THE SERMON TAKES LONGER THAN THIRTY MINUTES.	THE KISS HAS TOO MUCH TONGUE.	SOMEONE CRIES BEFORE, DURING & AFTER THE CEREMONY.
THE VOWS FEATURE A QUOTE FROM 'THE NOTEBOOK.'	THE OFFICIANT PRONOUNCES SOMEONE'S NAME WRONG.	THE COUPLE AWKWARDLY DANCES DOWN THE AISLE AFTER BEING ANNOUNCED.	A WILDLY UNDERDRESSED GUEST SHOWS UP.	THE BRIDE OR GROOM SAID THE WRONG NAME.
THE VOWS ARE WHISPERED AND HEARD BY ABSOLUTELY NO ONE.	SOMEONE STILL BRINGS A CHILD TO AN ADULT-ONLY WEDDING.	✕	TOO MUCH ENERGY IS SPENT KEEPING DIVORCED PARENTS APART.	THE RINGS ARE DROPPED.
A CHILD JUST LAYS DOWN IN THE MIDDLE OF THE STAGE.	THE BRIDAL PARTY IS DRESSED IN THE LEAST FLATTERING DRESSES.	A DOG IS IN THE WEDDING PARTY.	THE PROGRAM HAS MULTIPLE PAGES.	SOMEONE IS ALREADY DRINKING FROM A FLASK.
THE FLOWERS TRIGGERED ALLERGIES & SOMEONE CAN'T STOP SNEEZING.	THE WEDDING PROCESSION WALKS AT THE SPEED OF LIGHT.	A MEMBER OF THE WEDDING PARTY IS CURRENTLY INEBRIATED.	'FOR RICHER OR FOR RICHER.'	THE WHOLE THING LASTS FOR OVER TWO HOURS.

OBJECTIVE

OH, YOU MEAN BESIDES TRYING TO PASS THE TIME DURING THIS WEDDING THAT YOU MAY OR MAY NOT HAVE EVEN WANTED TO GO TO? ISN'T THAT ENOUGH? WHAT DO YOU WANT FROM US?

WELL, WE HOPE YOU'RE AT LEAST FAMILIAR WITH THE CONCEPT OF BINGO. BECAUSE IF NOT, WELL WE ARE REALLY KIND OF WORRIED ABOUT YOU. WHAT OTHER THINGS IN LIFE HAVE YOU MISSED? SHOES? AUTOMOBILES? TWO-PLY TOILET PAPER? WE DIGRESS.

THIS WEDDING BIN·GO GAME IS PLAYED MUCH LIKE THE TRADITIONAL ONE. YOUR GOAL IS TO SIMPLY BE THE FIRST TO FILL 5 SEQUENTIAL SQUARES IN A ROW, A COLUMN, OR EVEN DIAGONALLY (SEE FIGURE 1 BELOW).

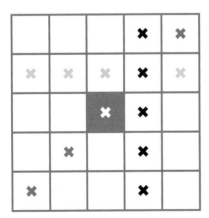

FIGURE 1

SEE THAT X IN THE CENTER SQUARE OF YOUR BOARDS? THAT'S A FREE SQUARE—WHICH MEANS EVERY PLAYER GETS THIS ONE AUTOMATICALLY. IT REALLY HELPS SO...YOU'RE WELCOME

PLAYING THE GAME

AFTER DETERMINING HOW MANY PEOPLE ARE PLAYING, THE OWNER OF THE BOOK SHOULD PERF. OUT A CARD (OR TWO) FOR EVERYONE TO USE AS THEIR PLAY BOARD(S).

ALRIGHT, SO HERE'S HOW OUR GAME IS A BIT DIFFERENT. WE'VE PRE-FILLED EACH CARD WITH THE COMMON (YET RIDICULOUS) THINGS THAT ALWAYS SEEM TO HAPPEN AT THESE EVENTS. SO, INSTEAD OF SOMEONE JUST CALLING OUT NUMBERS, EVERYONE IS PEOPLE WATCHING INSTEAD. WHEN SOMETHING HAPPENS THAT IS ON ONE OF YOUR SQUARES, YOU CALL IT OUT* (AS DISCREETLY AS APPROPRIATE, OF COURSE) AND MARK OFF THE SQUARE. JUST MAKE THE OTHER PLAYERS ARE AWARE.

BY THE WAY, BRIDES & GROOMS TEND TO DO UNIQUELY STUPID THINGS, SO WE PUT THEM IN. ATTENDING A SAME SEX MARRIAGE? AWESOME. FEEL FREE TO MODIFY THE SQUARES AS NEEDED.

WINNING

WHEN A PLAYER MARKS OFF A WINNING CARD, THEY SHOULD YELL* 'BINGO.' IN THE EVENT OF A TIE, THE FIRST TO SAY IT IS THE WINNER. EITHER WAY—EVERYONE ELSE IN THE ROOM WILL PROBABLY BE WONDERING WHAT THE HELL YOU ARE DOING. ADMITTEDLY IT MIGHT BE HARD TO MAKE A TRUE BINGO, SO YOU CAN ALSO DECIDE THAT THE PLAYER WITH THE MOST SQUARES MARKED OFF IS THE WINNER.

BONUS: YOU CAN ALSO PLAY THIS AS A DRINKING GAME. IT'S SIMPLE. WHEN SOMETHING HAPPENS ON YOUR CARD, YOU HAVE TO TAKE A DRINK. IF YOU MAKE A BINGO—WELL NOW EVERYONE ELSE HAS TO DRINK. JUST MAYBE WAIT UNTIL THE RECEPTION TO START DRINKING. THAT'S WHERE THE OPEN BAR IS ANYWAY.

*DON'T ACTUALLY YELL (OR TALK) DURING A WEDDING.

THERE'S A PROP IN THE CEREMONY. CANDLE, SAND, LIVE BIRDS, ETC.	THE BRIDE OR GROOM SAID THE WRONG NAME.	THE BRIDE TRIPS WHILE WALKING DOWN THE AISLE.	THE DRESS CODE IS CLEARLY JUST MADE-UP. I.E. "MOUNTAIN SEMI-CASUAL"	A WILDLY UNDERDRESSED GUEST SHOWS UP.
SOMEONE CRIES BEFORE, DURING & AFTER THE CEREMONY.	A MEMBER OF THE WEDDING PARTY IS CURRENTLY INEBRIATED.	THE VOWS TAKE AT LEAST 5 MINUTES, EACH.	A CHILD FACE-PLANTS BEFORE REACHING THE END OF THE AISLE	RING BEARER OR FLOWER GIRL CAN'T MAKE IT DOWN THE AISLE
SOMETHING IMPORTANT BLOWS AWAY DURING AN OUTDOOR CEREMONY.	THE RINGS ARE DROPPED.	✖	THE WHOLE THING LASTS FOR OVER TWO HOURS.	THE BRIDAL PARTY IS DRESSED IN THE LEAST FLATTERING DRESSES.
THE COUPLE AWKWARDLY DANCES DOWN THE AISLE AFTER BEING ANNOUNCED.	A MEMBER OF THE WEDDING PARTY IS OBVIOUSLY HUNGOVER.	THE WEDDING STARTS AT LEAST THIRTY MINUTES LATE	THE VOWS ARE WHISPERED AND HEARD BY ABSOLUTELY NO ONE	THE GROOMSMEN ARE ALL WEARING SUSPENDERS
SOMEONE ACTUALLY OBJECTS.	SOMEONE STILL BRINGS A CHILD TO AN ADULT-ONLY WEDDING.	SOMEONE IS CRYING SO LOUDLY YOU CAN'T HEAR THE VOWS.	"LOVE IS PATIENT, LOVE IS KIND."	A CLASSICAL VERSION OF A POP SONG IS USED FOR THE AISLE WALK

OBJECTIVE

OH, YOU MEAN BESIDES TRYING TO PASS THE TIME DURING THIS WEDDING THAT YOU MAY OR MAY NOT HAVE EVEN WANTED TO GO TO? ISN'T THAT ENOUGH? WHAT DO YOU WANT FROM US?

WELL, WE HOPE YOU'RE AT LEAST FAMILIAR WITH THE CONCEPT OF BINGO, BECAUSE IF NOT, WELL WE ARE REALLY KIND OF WORRIED ABOUT YOU, WHAT OTHER THINGS IN LIFE HAVE YOU MISSED? SHOES? AUTOMOBILES? TWO-PLY TOILET PAPER? WE DIGRESS.

THIS WEDDING BIN×GO GAME IS PLAYED MUCH LIKE THE TRADITIONAL ONE. YOUR GOAL IS TO SIMPLY BE THE FIRST TO FILL 5 SEQUENTIAL SQUARES IN A ROW, A COLUMN, OR EVEN DIAGONALLY (SEE FIGURE 1 BELOW).

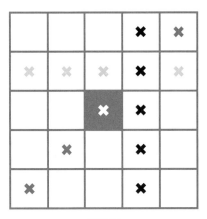

FIGURE 1

SEE THAT X IN THE CENTER SQUARE OF YOUR BOARDS? THAT'S A FREE SQUARE—WHICH MEANS EVERY PLAYER GETS THIS ONE AUTOMATICALLY. IT REALLY HELPS SO...YOU'RE WELCOME

PLAYING THE GAME

AFTER DETERMINING HOW MANY PEOPLE ARE PLAYING, THE OWNER OF THE BOOK SHOULD PERF. OUT A CARD (OR TWO) FOR EVERYONE TO USE AS THEIR PLAY BOARD(S).

ALRIGHT, SO HERE'S HOW OUR GAME IS A BIT DIFFERENT. WE'VE PRE-FILLED EACH CARD WITH THE COMMON (YET RIDICULOUS) THINGS THAT ALWAYS SEEM TO HAPPEN AT THESE EVENTS. SO, INSTEAD OF SOMEONE JUST CALLING OUT NUMBERS, EVERYONE IS PEOPLE WATCHING INSTEAD. WHEN SOMETHING HAPPENS THAT IS ON ONE OF YOUR SQUARES, YOU CALL IT OUT* (AS DISCREETLY AS APPROPRIATE, OF COURSE) AND MARK OFF THE SQUARE. JUST MAKE THE OTHER PLAYERS ARE AWARE.

BY THE WAY, BRIDES & GROOMS TEND TO DO UNIQUELY STUPID THINGS, SO WE PUT THEM IN. ATTENDING A SAME SEX MARRIAGE? AWESOME. FEEL FREE TO MODIFY THE SQUARES AS NEEDED.

WINNING

WHEN A PLAYER MARKS OFF A WINNING CARD, THEY SHOULD YELL* 'BINGO.' IN THE EVENT OF A TIE, THE FIRST TO SAY IT IS THE WINNER. EITHER WAY—EVERYONE ELSE IN THE ROOM WILL PROBABLY BE WONDERING WHAT THE HELL YOU ARE DOING. ADMITTEDLY IT MIGHT BE HARD TO MAKE A TRUE BINGO, SO YOU CAN ALSO DECIDE THAT THE PLAYER WITH THE MOST SQUARES MARKED OFF IS THE WINNER.

BONUS: YOU CAN ALSO PLAY THIS AS A DRINKING GAME. IT'S SIMPLE. WHEN SOMETHING HAPPENS ON YOUR CARD, YOU HAVE TO TAKE A DRINK. IF YOU MAKE A BINGO—WELL NOW EVERYONE ELSE HAS TO DRINK. JUST MAYBE WAIT UNTIL THE RECEPTION TO START DRINKING. THAT'S WHERE THE OPEN BAR IS ANYWAY.

*DON'T ACTUALLY YELL (OR TALK) DURING A WEDDING.

THE VOWS TAKE AT LEAST 5 MINUTES, EACH.	THE OFFICIANT PRONOUNCES SOMEONE'S NAME WRONG.	THERE'S A PROP IN THE CEREMONY. CANDLE, SAND, LIVE BIRDS, ETC.	SOMEONE MESSES UP THE VOWS	SOMEONE IS USING THE PROGRAM AS A FAN
EVERYONE AT THE ALTAR HAS THEIR OWN MICROPHONE.	THE MOTHER OF THE GROOM SPENDS MOST OF HER TIME GLARING AT THE BRIDE.	THE COUPLE AWKWARDLY DANCES DOWN THE AISLE AFTER BEING ANNOUNCED.	THE WHOLE THING LASTS FOR OVER TWO HOURS.	THE GROOMSMEN ARE ALL WEARING SUSPENDERS
SOMEONE IS ALREADY DRINKING FROM A FLASK.	THE FLOWERS TRIGGERED ALLERGIES & SOMEONE CAN'T STOP SNEEZING.	✖	A MEMBER OF THE WEDDING PARTY IS OBVIOUSLY HUNGOVER.	THE BRIDE OR GROOM SAID THE WRONG NAME
SOMEONE IS CRYING SO LOUDLY YOU CAN'T HEAR THE VOWS.	THE WEDDING PARTY IS STANDING IN ORDER OF SHORTEST TO TALLEST.	'FOR RICHER OR FOR RICHER.'	SOMEONE SINGS A HEARTFELT SONG. IT'S NOT IN KEY.	THE WEDDING PROCESSION WALKS AT THE SPEED OF LIGHT
THE VOWS FEATURE A QUOTE FROM 'THE NOTEBOOK.'	'LOVE IS PATIENT. LOVE IS KIND.'	THE SERMON TAKES LONGER THAN THIRTY MINUTES.	THE RINGS ARE FORGOTTEN AND/OR LOST.	TOO MUCH ENERGY IS SPENT KEEPING DIVORCED PARENTS APART.

OBJECTIVE

OH, YOU MEAN BESIDES TRYING TO PASS THE TIME DURING THIS WEDDING THAT YOU MAY OR MAY NOT HAVE EVEN WANTED TO GO TO? ISN'T THAT ENOUGH? WHAT DO YOU WANT FROM US?

WELL, WE HOPE YOU'RE AT LEAST FAMILIAR WITH THE CONCEPT OF BINGO. BECAUSE IF NOT, WELL WE ARE REALLY KIND OF WORRIED ABOUT YOU. WHAT OTHER THINGS IN LIFE HAVE YOU MISSED? SHOES? AUTOMOBILES? TWO-PLY TOILET PAPER? WE DIGRESS.

THIS WEDDING BIN×GO GAME IS PLAYED MUCH LIKE THE TRADITIONAL ONE. YOUR GOAL IS TO SIMPLY BE THE FIRST TO FILL 5 SEQUENTIAL SQUARES IN A ROW, A COLUMN, OR EVEN DIAGONALLY (SEE FIGURE 1 BELOW).

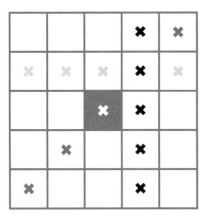

FIGURE 1

SEE THAT X IN THE CENTER SQUARE OF YOUR BOARDS? THAT'S A FREE SQUARE—WHICH MEANS EVERY PLAYER GETS THIS ONE AUTOMATICALLY. IT REALLY HELPS SO...YOU'RE WELCOME

PLAYING THE GAME

AFTER DETERMINING HOW MANY PEOPLE ARE PLAYING, THE OWNER OF THE BOOK SHOULD PERF. OUT A CARD (OR TWO) FOR EVERYONE TO USE AS THEIR PLAY BOARD(S).

ALRIGHT, SO HERE'S HOW OUR GAME IS A BIT DIFFERENT. WE'VE PRE-FILLED EACH CARD WITH THE COMMON (YET RIDICULOUS) THINGS THAT ALWAYS SEEM TO HAPPEN AT THESE EVENTS. SO, INSTEAD OF SOMEONE JUST CALLING OUT NUMBERS, EVERYONE IS PEOPLE WATCHING INSTEAD. WHEN SOMETHING HAPPENS THAT IS ON ONE OF YOUR SQUARES, YOU CALL IT OUT* (AS DISCREETLY AS APPROPRIATE, OF COURSE) AND MARK OFF THE SQUARE. JUST MAKE THE OTHER PLAYERS ARE AWARE.

BY THE WAY, BRIDES & GROOMS TEND TO DO UNIQUELY STUPID THINGS, SO WE PUT THEM IN. ATTENDING A SAME SEX MARRIAGE? AWESOME. FEEL FREE TO MODIFY THE SQUARES AS NEEDED.

WINNING

WHEN A PLAYER MARKS OFF A WINNING CARD, THEY SHOULD YELL* 'BINGO.' IN THE EVENT OF A TIE, THE FIRST TO SAY IT IS THE WINNER. EITHER WAY—EVERYONE ELSE IN THE ROOM WILL PROBABLY BE WONDERING WHAT THE HELL YOU ARE DOING. ADMITTEDLY IT MIGHT BE HARD TO MAKE A TRUE BINGO, SO YOU CAN ALSO DECIDE THAT THE PLAYER WITH THE MOST SQUARES MARKED OFF IS THE WINNER.

BONUS: YOU CAN ALSO PLAY THIS AS A DRINKING GAME. IT'S SIMPLE. WHEN SOMETHING HAPPENS ON YOUR CARD, YOU HAVE TO TAKE A DRINK. IF YOU MAKE A BINGO—WELL NOW EVERYONE ELSE HAS TO DRINK. JUST MAYBE WAIT UNTIL THE RECEPTION TO START DRINKING. THAT'S WHERE THE OPEN BAR IS ANYWAY.

*DON'T ACTUALLY YELL (OR TALK) DURING A WEDDING.

WEDDING BIN×GO WEDDING

AN AUDIENCE MEMBER HAS CLEARLY FALLEN ASLEEP.	THE VOWS FEATURE A QUOTE FROM 'THE NOTEBOOK.'	EVERYONE AT THE ALTAR HAS THEIR OWN MICROPHONE.	YOU HAVE TO STAND UP & SIT DOWN ROUGHLY 100 TIMES.	'LOVE IS PATIENT, LOVE IS KIND.'
A CHILD JUST LAYS DOWN IN THE MIDDLE OF THE STAGE.	RING BEARER OR FLOWER GIRL CAN'T MAKE IT DOWN THE AISLE.	THE COUPLE AWKWARDLY DANCES DOWN THE AISLE AFTER BEING ANNOUNCED.	THE BRIDE IS WEARING 'QUIRKY' SHOES.	SOMEONE SINGS A HEARTFELT SONG, IT'S NOT IN KEY.
SOMEONE IS CRYING SO LOUDLY YOU CAN'T HEAR THE VOWS.	THE DRESS CODE IS CLEARLY JUST MADE-UP. I.E. 'MOUNTAIN SEMI-CASUAL'	✖	THE WEDDING PROCESSION WALKS AT THE SPEED OF LIGHT.	SOMEONE ACTUALLY OBJECTS.
THE SERMON TAKES LONGER THAN THIRTY MINUTES.	THE RINGS ARE FORGOTTEN AND/OR LOST.	THE VOWS ARE WHISPERED AND HEARD BY ABSOLUTELY NO ONE.	A DOG IS IN THE WEDDING PARTY.	A CLASSICAL VERSION OF A POP SONG IS USED FOR THE AISLE WALK.
THE OFFICIANT PRONOUNCES SOMEONE'S NAME WRONG.	THE WHOLE THING LASTS FOR OVER TWO HOURS.	SOMEONE STILL BRINGS A CHILD TO AN ADULT-ONLY WEDDING.	SOMEONE IS USING THE PROGRAM AS A FAN.	SOMETHING IMPORTANT BLOWS AWAY DURING AN OUTDOOR CEREMONY.

OBJECTIVE

OH, YOU MEAN BESIDES TRYING TO PASS THE TIME DURING THIS WEDDING THAT YOU MAY OR MAY NOT HAVE EVEN WANTED TO GO TO? ISN'T THAT ENOUGH? WHAT DO YOU WANT FROM US?

WELL, WE HOPE YOU'RE AT LEAST FAMILIAR WITH THE CONCEPT OF BINGO. BECAUSE IF NOT, WELL WE ARE REALLY KIND OF WORRIED ABOUT YOU. WHAT OTHER THINGS IN LIFE HAVE YOU MISSED? SHOES? AUTOMOBILES? TWO-PLY TOILET PAPER? WE DIGRESS.

THIS WEDDING BIN×GO GAME IS PLAYED MUCH LIKE THE TRADITIONAL ONE. YOUR GOAL IS TO SIMPLY BE THE FIRST TO FILL 5 SEQUENTIAL SQUARES IN A ROW, A COLUMN, OR EVEN DIAGONALLY (SEE FIGURE 1 BELOW).

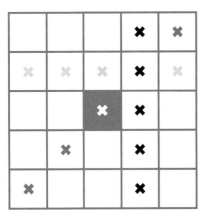

FIGURE 1

SEE THAT X IN THE CENTER SQUARE OF YOUR BOARDS? THAT'S A FREE SQUARE—WHICH MEANS EVERY PLAYER GETS THIS ONE AUTOMATICALLY. IT REALLY HELPS SO...YOU'RE WELCOME

PLAYING THE GAME

AFTER DETERMINING HOW MANY PEOPLE ARE PLAYING, THE OWNER OF THE BOOK SHOULD PERF. OUT A CARD (OR TWO) FOR EVERYONE TO USE AS THEIR PLAY BOARD(S).

ALRIGHT, SO HERE'S HOW OUR GAME IS A BIT DIFFERENT. WE'VE PRE-FILLED EACH CARD WITH THE COMMON (YET RIDICULOUS) THINGS THAT ALWAYS SEEM TO HAPPEN AT THESE EVENTS. SO, INSTEAD OF SOMEONE JUST CALLING OUT NUMBERS, EVERYONE IS PEOPLE WATCHING INSTEAD. WHEN SOMETHING HAPPENS THAT IS ON ONE OF YOUR SQUARES, YOU CALL IT OUT* (AS DISCREETLY AS APPROPRIATE, OF COURSE) AND MARK OFF THE SQUARE. JUST MAKE THE OTHER PLAYERS ARE AWARE.

BY THE WAY, BRIDES & GROOMS TEND TO DO UNIQUELY STUPID THINGS, SO WE PUT THEM IN. ATTENDING A SAME SEX MARRIAGE? AWESOME. FEEL FREE TO MODIFY THE SQUARES AS NEEDED.

WINNING

WHEN A PLAYER MARKS OFF A WINNING CARD, THEY SHOULD YELL**'BINGO.' IN THE EVENT OF A TIE, THE FIRST TO SAY IT IS THE WINNER. EITHER WAY—EVERYONE ELSE IN THE ROOM WILL PROBABLY BE WONDERING WHAT THE HELL YOU ARE DOING. ADMITTEDLY IT MIGHT BE HARD TO MAKE A TRUE BINGO, SO YOU CAN ALSO DECIDE THAT THE PLAYER WITH THE MOST SQUARES MARKED OFF IS THE WINNER.

BONUS: YOU CAN ALSO PLAY THIS AS A DRINKING GAME. IT'S SIMPLE. WHEN SOMETHING HAPPENS ON YOUR CARD, YOU HAVE TO TAKE A DRINK. IF YOU MAKE A BINGO—WELL NOW EVERYONE ELSE HAS TO DRINK. JUST MAYBE WAIT UNTIL THE RECEPTION TO START DRINKING. THAT'S WHERE THE OPEN BAR IS ANYWAY.

*DON'T ACTUALLY YELL (OR TALK) DURING A WEDDING.

BIN×GO

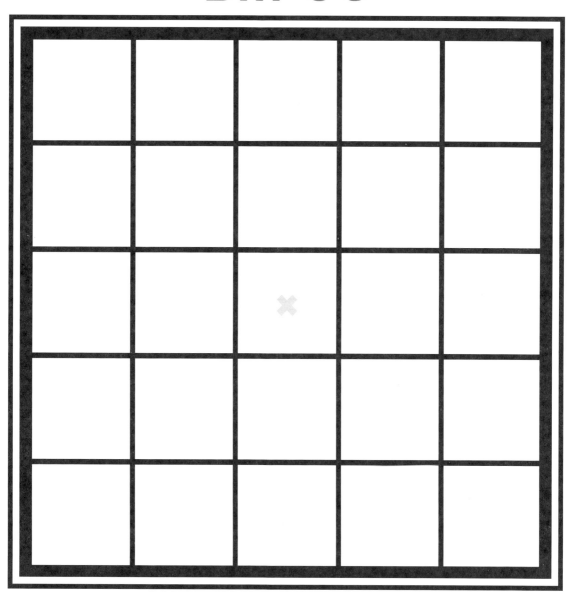

OBJECTIVE

THIS TIME, IT'S PERSONAL—LITERALLY. YOU KNOW YOUR FAMILY & FRIENDS BEST, SO USE THESE SIX CARDS TO CREATE YOUR OWN HIGHLY SPECIFIC BINGO GAME. DOES YOUR GREAT UNCLE KARL ALWAYS BREAK OUT HIS HARMONICA AFTER A FEW COCKTAILS? WELL, YOU SHOULD FILL A SQUARE WITH IT. CREATE A GAME FOR THE RECEPTION, THE WEDDING, OR SOMETHING ELSE ENTIRELY. WE'LL LEAVE THAT UP TO YOU. YOU PURCHASED THIS BOOK AFTER ALL, IT'S THE LEAST WE COULD DO.

REGARDLESS, THIS BIN·GO GAME IS PLAYED MUCH LIKE THE TRADITIONAL ONE. YOUR GOAL IS TO SIMPLY BE THE FIRST TO FILL FIVE SEQUENTIAL SQUARES IN A ROW, A COLUMN, OR EVEN DIAGONALLY (SEE FIGURE 1 BELOW).

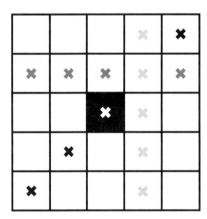

FIGURE 1

SEE THAT X IN THE CENTER SQUARE OF YOUR BOARDS? THAT'S A FREE SQUARE—WHICH MEANS EVERY PLAYER GETS THIS ONE AUTOMATICALLY. IT REALLY HELPS SO...YOU'RE WELCOME

PLAYING THE GAME

AFTER DETERMINING HOW MANY PEOPLE ARE PLAYING, THE OWNER OF THE BOOK SHOULD PERF. OUT THE CARDS AND FILL THE SQUARES WITH PERSONALIZED 'CLICHÉS'—JUST MAKE SURE EACH BOARD IS DIFFERENT. WORK AS A GROUP, OR CREATE ALL OF THE SQUARES YOURSELF AHEAD OF TIME. IT'S FUN, TRUST US.

ALRIGHT, SO HERE'S HOW OUR GAME IS A BIT DIFFERENT. INSTEAD OF SOMEONE JUST CALLING OUT NUMBERS, EVERYONE IS PEOPLE WATCHING INSTEAD. WHEN SOMETHING HAPPENS THAT IS ON ONE OF YOUR SQUARES, YOU CALL IT OUT (AS DISCREETLY AS APPROPRIATE, OF COURSE) AND MARK OFF THE SQUARE.

JUST REMEMBER THAT THE OTHER PLAYERS NEED TO BE AWARE OF THE 'CALL'—AND IDEALLY SEE IT AS WELL (BUT THAT'S NOT A REQUIREMENT). THAT WAY THEY CAN ALSO MARK OFF THAT SQUARE IF IT'S ON THEIR BOARD.

WINNING

WHEN A PLAYER MARKS OFF A WINNING CARD, THEY SHOULD YELL* 'BINGO.' IN THE EVENT OF A TIE, THE FIRST TO SAY IT IS THE WINNER. EITHER WAY—EVERYONE ELSE IN THE ROOM WILL PROBABLY BE WONDERING WHAT THE HELL YOU ARE DOING. ADMITTEDLY IT MIGHT BE HARD TO MAKE A TRUE BINGO, SO YOU CAN ALSO DECIDE THAT THE PLAYER WITH THE MOST SQUARES MARKED OFF IS THE WINNER.

BONUS: YOU CAN ALSO PLAY THIS AS A DRINKING GAME. IT'S SIMPLE. WHEN SOMETHING HAPPENS ON YOUR CARD, YOU HAVE TO TAKE A DRINK. (YOU'RE PROBABLY DOING THAT ANYWAY AFTER ALL). BUT IF YOU MAKE A BINGO—WELL NOW EVERYONE ELSE HAS TO DRINK. JUST BE RESPONSIBLE OF COURSE.

*DON'T ACTUALLY YELL (OR TALK) DURING A WEDDING.

BIN×GO

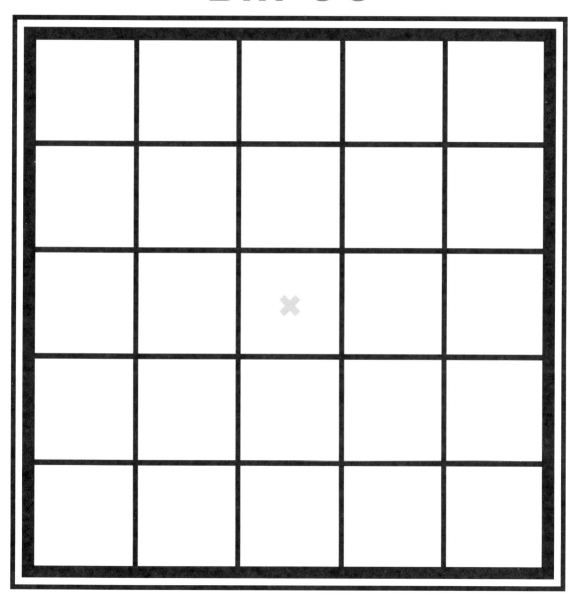

OBJECTIVE

THIS TIME, IT'S PERSONAL—LITERALLY. YOU KNOW YOUR FAMILY & FRIENDS BEST, SO USE THESE SIX CARDS TO CREATE YOUR OWN HIGHLY SPECIFIC BINGO GAME. DOES YOUR GREAT UNCLE KARL ALWAYS BREAK OUT HIS HARMONICA AFTER A FEW COCKTAILS? WELL, YOU SHOULD FILL A SQUARE WITH IT. CREATE A GAME FOR THE RECEPTION, THE WEDDING, OR SOMETHING ELSE ENTIRELY. WE'LL LEAVE THAT UP TO YOU. YOU PURCHASED THIS BOOK AFTER ALL, IT'S THE LEAST WE COULD DO.

REGARDLESS, THIS BIN·GO GAME IS PLAYED MUCH LIKE THE TRADITIONAL ONE. YOUR GOAL IS TO SIMPLY BE THE FIRST TO FILL FIVE SEQUENTIAL SQUARES IN A ROW, A COLUMN, OR EVEN DIAGONALLY (SEE FIGURE 1 BELOW).

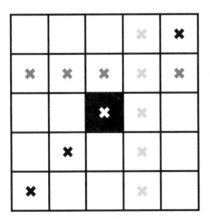

FIGURE 1

SEE THAT X IN THE CENTER SQUARE OF YOUR BOARDS? THAT'S A FREE SQUARE—WHICH MEANS EVERY PLAYER GETS THIS ONE AUTOMATICALLY. IT REALLY HELPS SO...YOU'RE WELCOME

PLAYING THE GAME

AFTER DETERMINING HOW MANY PEOPLE ARE PLAYING, THE OWNER OF THE BOOK SHOULD PERF. OUT THE CARDS AND FILL THE SQUARES WITH PERSONALIZED 'CLICHÉS'—JUST MAKE SURE EACH BOARD IS DIFFERENT. WORK AS A GROUP, OR CREATE ALL OF THE SQUARES YOURSELF AHEAD OF TIME. IT'S FUN, TRUST US.

ALRIGHT, SO HERE'S HOW OUR GAME IS A BIT DIFFERENT. INSTEAD OF SOMEONE JUST CALLING OUT NUMBERS, EVERYONE IS PEOPLE WATCHING INSTEAD. WHEN SOMETHING HAPPENS THAT IS ON ONE OF YOUR SQUARES, YOU CALL IT OUT (AS DISCREETLY AS APPROPRIATE, OF COURSE) AND MARK OFF THE SQUARE.

JUST REMEMBER THAT THE OTHER PLAYERS NEED TO BE AWARE OF THE 'CALL'—AND IDEALLY SEE IT AS WELL (BUT THAT'S NOT A REQUIREMENT). THAT WAY THEY CAN ALSO MARK OFF THAT SQUARE IF IT'S ON THEIR BOARD.

WINNING

WHEN A PLAYER MARKS OFF A WINNING CARD, THEY SHOULD YELL* 'BINGO.' IN THE EVENT OF A TIE, THE FIRST TO SAY IT IS THE WINNER. EITHER WAY—EVERYONE ELSE IN THE ROOM WILL PROBABLY BE WONDERING WHAT THE HELL YOU ARE DOING. ADMITTEDLY IT MIGHT BE HARD TO MAKE A TRUE BINGO, SO YOU CAN ALSO DECIDE THAT THE PLAYER WITH THE MOST SQUARES MARKED OFF IS THE WINNER.

BONUS: YOU CAN ALSO PLAY THIS AS A DRINKING GAME. IT'S SIMPLE. WHEN SOMETHING HAPPENS ON YOUR CARD, YOU HAVE TO TAKE A DRINK. (YOU'RE PROBABLY DOING THAT ANYWAY AFTER ALL). BUT IF YOU MAKE A BINGO—WELL NOW EVERYONE ELSE HAS TO DRINK. JUST BE RESPONSIBLE OF COURSE.

*DON'T ACTUALLY YELL (OR TALK) DURING A WEDDING.

BIN×GO

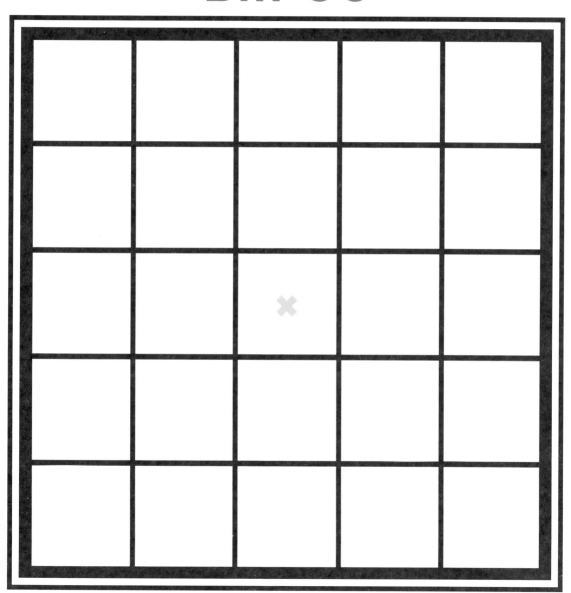

OBJECTIVE

THIS TIME, IT'S PERSONAL—LITERALLY. YOU KNOW YOUR FAMILY & FRIENDS BEST, SO USE THESE SIX CARDS TO CREATE YOUR OWN HIGHLY SPECIFIC BINGO GAME. DOES YOUR GREAT UNCLE KARL ALWAYS BREAK OUT HIS HARMONICA AFTER A FEW COCKTAILS? WELL, YOU SHOULD FILL A SQUARE WITH IT. CREATE A GAME FOR THE RECEPTION, THE WEDDING, OR SOMETHING ELSE ENTIRELY. WE'LL LEAVE THAT UP TO YOU. YOU PURCHASED THIS BOOK AFTER ALL, IT'S THE LEAST WE COULD DO.

REGARDLESS, THIS BIN·GO GAME IS PLAYED MUCH LIKE THE TRADITIONAL ONE. YOUR GOAL IS TO SIMPLY BE THE FIRST TO FILL FIVE SEQUENTIAL SQUARES IN A ROW, A COLUMN, OR EVEN DIAGONALLY (SEE FIGURE 1 BELOW).

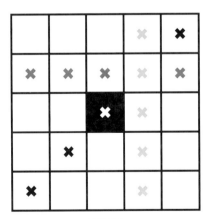

FIGURE 1

SEE THAT X IN THE CENTER SQUARE OF YOUR BOARDS? THAT'S A FREE SQUARE—WHICH MEANS EVERY PLAYER GETS THIS ONE AUTOMATICALLY. IT REALLY HELPS SO...YOU'RE WELCOME

PLAYING THE GAME

AFTER DETERMINING HOW MANY PEOPLE ARE PLAYING, THE OWNER OF THE BOOK SHOULD PERF. OUT THE CARDS AND FILL THE SQUARES WITH PERSONALIZED 'CLICHÉS'—JUST MAKE SURE EACH BOARD IS DIFFERENT. WORK AS A GROUP, OR CREATE ALL OF THE SQUARES YOURSELF AHEAD OF TIME. IT'S FUN, TRUST US.

ALRIGHT, SO HERE'S HOW OUR GAME IS A BIT DIFFERENT. INSTEAD OF SOMEONE JUST CALLING OUT NUMBERS, EVERYONE IS PEOPLE WATCHING INSTEAD. WHEN SOMETHING HAPPENS THAT IS ON ONE OF YOUR SQUARES, YOU CALL IT OUT (AS DISCREETLY AS APPROPRIATE, OF COURSE) AND MARK OFF THE SQUARE.

JUST REMEMBER THAT THE OTHER PLAYERS NEED TO BE AWARE OF THE 'CALL'—AND IDEALLY SEE IT AS WELL (BUT THAT'S NOT A REQUIREMENT). THAT WAY THEY CAN ALSO MARK OFF THAT SQUARE IF IT'S ON THEIR BOARD.

WINNING

WHEN A PLAYER MARKS OFF A WINNING CARD, THEY SHOULD YELL* 'BINGO.' IN THE EVENT OF A TIE, THE FIRST TO SAY IT IS THE WINNER. EITHER WAY—EVERYONE ELSE IN THE ROOM WILL PROBABLY BE WONDERING WHAT THE HELL YOU ARE DOING. ADMITTEDLY IT MIGHT BE HARD TO MAKE A TRUE BINGO, SO YOU CAN ALSO DECIDE THAT THE PLAYER WITH THE MOST SQUARES MARKED OFF IS THE WINNER.

BONUS: YOU CAN ALSO PLAY THIS AS A DRINKING GAME. IT'S SIMPLE. WHEN SOMETHING HAPPENS ON YOUR CARD, YOU HAVE TO TAKE A DRINK. (YOU'RE PROBABLY DOING THAT ANYWAY AFTER ALL). BUT IF YOU MAKE A BINGO—WELL NOW EVERYONE ELSE HAS TO DRINK. JUST BE RESPONSIBLE OF COURSE.

*DON'T ACTUALLY YELL (OR TALK) DURING A WEDDING.

PERSONALIZED **BIN×GO** PERSONALIZED

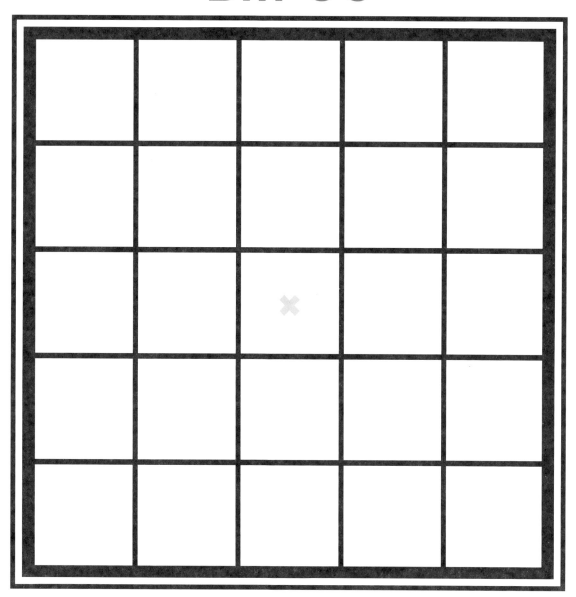

OBJECTIVE

THIS TIME, IT'S PERSONAL—LITERALLY. YOU KNOW YOUR FAMILY & FRIENDS BEST, SO USE THESE SIX CARDS TO CREATE YOUR OWN HIGHLY SPECIFIC BINGO GAME. DOES YOUR GREAT UNCLE KARL ALWAYS BREAK OUT HIS HARMONICA AFTER A FEW COCKTAILS? WELL, YOU SHOULD FILL A SQUARE WITH IT. CREATE A GAME FOR THE RECEPTION, THE WEDDING, OR SOMETHING ELSE ENTIRELY. WE'LL LEAVE THAT UP TO YOU. YOU PURCHASED THIS BOOK AFTER ALL, IT'S THE LEAST WE COULD DO.

REGARDLESS, THIS BIN×GO GAME IS PLAYED MUCH LIKE THE TRADITIONAL ONE. YOUR GOAL IS TO SIMPLY BE THE FIRST TO FILL FIVE SEQUENTIAL SQUARES IN A ROW, A COLUMN, OR EVEN DIAGONALLY (SEE FIGURE 1 BELOW).

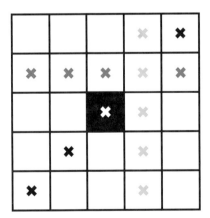

FIGURE 1

SEE THAT X IN THE CENTER SQUARE OF YOUR BOARDS? THAT'S A FREE SQUARE—WHICH MEANS EVERY PLAYER GETS THIS ONE AUTOMATICALLY. IT REALLY HELPS SO...YOU'RE WELCOME

PLAYING THE GAME

AFTER DETERMINING HOW MANY PEOPLE ARE PLAYING, THE OWNER OF THE BOOK SHOULD PERF. OUT THE CARDS AND FILL THE SQUARES WITH PERSONALIZED 'CLICHÉS'—JUST MAKE SURE EACH BOARD IS DIFFERENT. WORK AS A GROUP, OR CREATE ALL OF THE SQUARES YOURSELF AHEAD OF TIME. IT'S FUN, TRUST US.

ALRIGHT, SO HERE'S HOW OUR GAME IS A BIT DIFFERENT. INSTEAD OF SOMEONE JUST CALLING OUT NUMBERS, EVERYONE IS PEOPLE WATCHING INSTEAD. WHEN SOMETHING HAPPENS THAT IS ON ONE OF YOUR SQUARES, YOU CALL IT OUT (AS DISCREETLY AS APPROPRIATE, OF COURSE) AND MARK OFF THE SQUARE.

JUST REMEMBER THAT THE OTHER PLAYERS NEED TO BE AWARE OF THE 'CALL'—AND IDEALLY SEE IT AS WELL (BUT THAT'S NOT A REQUIREMENT). THAT WAY THEY CAN ALSO MARK OFF THAT SQUARE IF IT'S ON THEIR BOARD.

WINNING

WHEN A PLAYER MARKS OFF A WINNING CARD, THEY SHOULD YELL* 'BINGO.' IN THE EVENT OF A TIE, THE FIRST TO SAY IT IS THE WINNER. EITHER WAY—EVERYONE ELSE IN THE ROOM WILL PROBABLY BE WONDERING WHAT THE HELL YOU ARE DOING. ADMITTEDLY IT MIGHT BE HARD TO MAKE A TRUE BINGO, SO YOU CAN ALSO DECIDE THAT THE PLAYER WITH THE MOST SQUARES MARKED OFF IS THE WINNER.

BONUS: YOU CAN ALSO PLAY THIS AS A DRINKING GAME. IT'S SIMPLE. WHEN SOMETHING HAPPENS ON YOUR CARD, YOU HAVE TO TAKE A DRINK. (YOU'RE PROBABLY DOING THAT ANYWAY AFTER ALL). BUT IF YOU MAKE A BINGO—WELL NOW EVERYONE ELSE HAS TO DRINK. JUST BE RESPONSIBLE OF COURSE.

*DON'T ACTUALLY YELL (OR TALK) DURING A WEDDING.

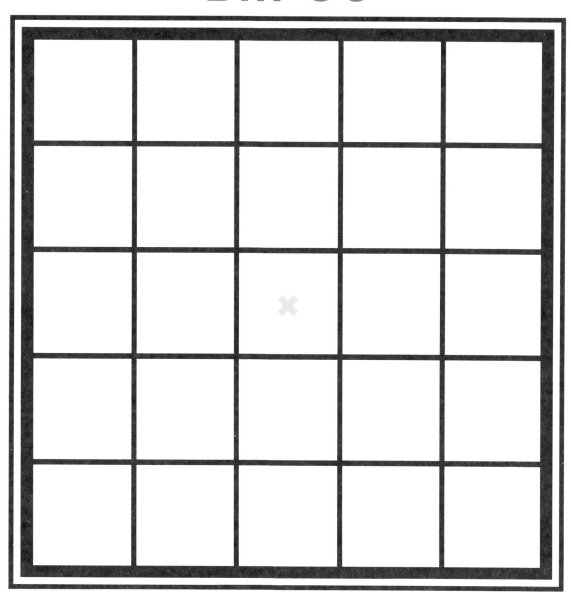

OBJECTIVE

THIS TIME, IT'S PERSONAL—LITERALLY. YOU KNOW YOUR FAMILY & FRIENDS BEST, SO USE THESE SIX CARDS TO CREATE YOUR OWN HIGHLY SPECIFIC BINGO GAME. DOES YOUR GREAT UNCLE KARL ALWAYS BREAK OUT HIS HARMONICA AFTER A FEW COCKTAILS? WELL, YOU SHOULD FILL A SQUARE WITH IT. CREATE A GAME FOR THE RECEPTION, THE WEDDING, OR SOMETHING ELSE ENTIRELY. WE'LL LEAVE THAT UP TO YOU. YOU PURCHASED THIS BOOK AFTER ALL, IT'S THE LEAST WE COULD DO.

REGARDLESS, THIS BIN·GO GAME IS PLAYED MUCH LIKE THE TRADITIONAL ONE. YOUR GOAL IS TO SIMPLY BE THE FIRST TO FILL FIVE SEQUENTIAL SQUARES IN A ROW, A COLUMN, OR EVEN DIAGONALLY (SEE FIGURE 1 BELOW).

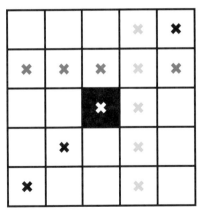

FIGURE 1

SEE THAT X IN THE CENTER SQUARE OF YOUR BOARDS? THAT'S A FREE SQUARE—WHICH MEANS EVERY PLAYER GETS THIS ONE AUTOMATICALLY. IT REALLY HELPS SO...YOU'RE WELCOME

PLAYING THE GAME

AFTER DETERMINING HOW MANY PEOPLE ARE PLAYING, THE OWNER OF THE BOOK SHOULD PERF. OUT THE CARDS AND FILL THE SQUARES WITH PERSONALIZED 'CLICHÉS'—JUST MAKE SURE EACH BOARD IS DIFFERENT. WORK AS A GROUP, OR CREATE ALL OF THE SQUARES YOURSELF AHEAD OF TIME. IT'S FUN, TRUST US.

ALRIGHT, SO HERE'S HOW OUR GAME IS A BIT DIFFERENT. INSTEAD OF SOMEONE JUST CALLING OUT NUMBERS, EVERYONE IS PEOPLE WATCHING INSTEAD. WHEN SOMETHING HAPPENS THAT IS ON ONE OF YOUR SQUARES, YOU CALL IT OUT (AS DISCREETLY AS APPROPRIATE, OF COURSE) AND MARK OFF THE SQUARE.

JUST REMEMBER THAT THE OTHER PLAYERS NEED TO BE AWARE OF THE 'CALL'—AND IDEALLY SEE IT AS WELL (BUT THAT'S NOT A REQUIREMENT). THAT WAY THEY CAN ALSO MARK OFF THAT SQUARE IF IT'S ON THEIR BOARD.

WINNING

WHEN A PLAYER MARKS OFF A WINNING CARD, THEY SHOULD YELL* 'BINGO.' IN THE EVENT OF A TIE, THE FIRST TO SAY IT IS THE WINNER. EITHER WAY—EVERYONE ELSE IN THE ROOM WILL PROBABLY BE WONDERING WHAT THE HELL YOU ARE DOING. ADMITTEDLY IT MIGHT BE HARD TO MAKE A TRUE BINGO, SO YOU CAN ALSO DECIDE THAT THE PLAYER WITH THE MOST SQUARES MARKED OFF IS THE WINNER.

BONUS: YOU CAN ALSO PLAY THIS AS A DRINKING GAME. IT'S SIMPLE. WHEN SOMETHING HAPPENS ON YOUR CARD, YOU HAVE TO TAKE A DRINK. (YOU'RE PROBABLY DOING THAT ANYWAY AFTER ALL). BUT IF YOU MAKE A BINGO—WELL NOW EVERYONE ELSE HAS TO DRINK. JUST BE RESPONSIBLE OF COURSE.

*DON'T ACTUALLY YELL (OR TALK) DURING A WEDDING.

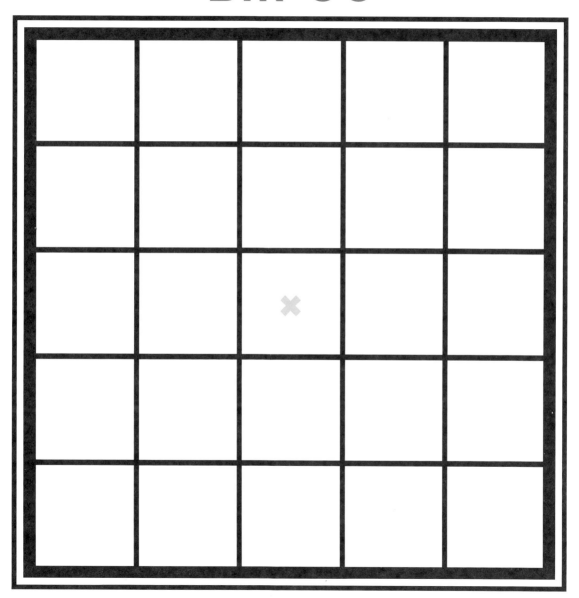

OBJECTIVE

THIS TIME, IT'S PERSONAL—LITERALLY. YOU KNOW YOUR FAMILY & FRIENDS BEST, SO USE THESE SIX CARDS TO CREATE YOUR OWN HIGHLY SPECIFIC BINGO GAME. DOES YOUR GREAT UNCLE KARL ALWAYS BREAK OUT HIS HARMONICA AFTER A FEW COCKTAILS? WELL, YOU SHOULD FILL A SQUARE WITH IT. CREATE A GAME FOR THE RECEPTION, THE WEDDING, OR SOMETHING ELSE ENTIRELY. WE'LL LEAVE THAT UP TO YOU. YOU PURCHASED THIS BOOK AFTER ALL, IT'S THE LEAST WE COULD DO.

REGARDLESS, THIS BIN·GO GAME IS PLAYED MUCH LIKE THE TRADITIONAL ONE. YOUR GOAL IS TO SIMPLY BE THE FIRST TO FILL FIVE SEQUENTIAL SQUARES IN A ROW, A COLUMN, OR EVEN DIAGONALLY (SEE FIGURE 1 BELOW).

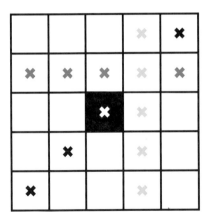

FIGURE 1

SEE THAT X IN THE CENTER SQUARE OF YOUR BOARDS? THAT'S A FREE SQUARE—WHICH MEANS EVERY PLAYER GETS THIS ONE AUTOMATICALLY. IT REALLY HELPS SO...YOU'RE WELCOME

PLAYING THE GAME

AFTER DETERMINING HOW MANY PEOPLE ARE PLAYING, THE OWNER OF THE BOOK SHOULD PERF. OUT THE CARDS AND FILL THE SQUARES WITH PERSONALIZED 'CLICHÉS'—JUST MAKE SURE EACH BOARD IS DIFFERENT. WORK AS A GROUP, OR CREATE ALL OF THE SQUARES YOURSELF AHEAD OF TIME. IT'S FUN, TRUST US.

ALRIGHT, SO HERE'S HOW OUR GAME IS A BIT DIFFERENT. INSTEAD OF SOMEONE JUST CALLING OUT NUMBERS, EVERYONE IS PEOPLE WATCHING INSTEAD. WHEN SOMETHING HAPPENS THAT IS ON ONE OF YOUR SQUARES, YOU CALL IT OUT (AS DISCREETLY AS APPROPRIATE, OF COURSE) AND MARK OFF THE SQUARE.

JUST REMEMBER THAT THE OTHER PLAYERS NEED TO BE AWARE OF THE 'CALL'—AND IDEALLY SEE IT AS WELL (BUT THAT'S NOT A REQUIREMENT). THAT WAY THEY CAN ALSO MARK OFF THAT SQUARE IF IT'S ON THEIR BOARD.

WINNING

WHEN A PLAYER MARKS OFF A WINNING CARD, THEY SHOULD YELL* 'BINGO.' IN THE EVENT OF A TIE, THE FIRST TO SAY IT IS THE WINNER. EITHER WAY—EVERYONE ELSE IN THE ROOM WILL PROBABLY BE WONDERING WHAT THE HELL YOU ARE DOING. ADMITTEDLY IT MIGHT BE HARD TO MAKE A TRUE BINGO, SO YOU CAN ALSO DECIDE THAT THE PLAYER WITH THE MOST SQUARES MARKED OFF IS THE WINNER.

BONUS: YOU CAN ALSO PLAY THIS AS A DRINKING GAME. IT'S SIMPLE. WHEN SOMETHING HAPPENS ON YOUR CARD, YOU HAVE TO TAKE A DRINK. (YOU'RE PROBABLY DOING THAT ANYWAY AFTER ALL). BUT IF YOU MAKE A BINGO—WELL NOW EVERYONE ELSE HAS TO DRINK. JUST BE RESPONSIBLE OF COURSE.

*DON'T ACTUALLY YELL (OR TALK) DURING A WEDDING.